£1·95

D1494807

ANOUILH:
ANTIGONE

W. D. HOWARTH
Professor of Classical French Literature, University of Bristol

EDWARD ARNOLD

© W. D. Howarth 1983

First published in Great Britain 1983
by Edward Arnold (Publishers) Ltd
41 Bedford Square
London WC1B 3DQ

Edward Arnold (Australia) Pty Ltd
80 Waverley Road
Caulfield East
Victoria 3145

British Library Cataloguing in Publication Data

Howarth, W. D.
    Anouilh: Antigone.—(Studies in French literature:
    no. 33)
    1. Anouilh, Jean. Antigone
    I. Title.   II. Series
    842'.912   PQ2601.N67Z/

    ISBN 0-7131-6394-1

Text set in 10/11 pt Bembo Compugraphic
by Colset Private Limited, Singapore
Printed and Bound in Great Britain
by The Camelot Press, Southampton

Contents

I Introduction

Jean Anouilh's career as a prolific, and highly successful, playwright extends over more than half a century. During virtually the whole of the period since his first play, *L'Hermine*, appeared in 1931, his thirty-odd new productions have been eagerly received by the theatregoing public; yet compared with certain other contemporary dramatists, Anouilh has been poorly regarded throughout his career by the critical establishment in France. Good interpretative studies of his work have appeared in England, in the United States and in Germany during the whole of this period; but academic criticism in France has almost completely ignored him, especially during the second half of his career. There is indeed a striking contrast between his fortunes in this respect and the critical attention accorded during the same period on the one hand to a philosopher-dramatist like Sartre, and on the other to such representatives of the Theatre of the Absurd as Beckett, Ionesco, Genet or Arrabal. If one may venture a controversial opinion at the outset, it seems to me that there are several of Anouilh's plays that offer a much better bet for probable survival into the twenty-first century than most of the works currently praised by the critical cognoscenti; in the meantime, the author of *Antigone* has proved well able to look after his own interests in satirical vein, for instance taking the academic critics on in their own idiom in *Le Songe du critique* (1960), and producing a devastating parody of the Theatre of the Absurd in *L'Hurluberlu* (1956), where a pretentious young poet gives a reading of 'Zim! Boum! ou Julien l'Apostat. Antidrame' by an avant-garde playwright with the splendidly evocative name of Popopief. The quality which I am sure will enable some at least of Anouilh's plays to outlive those of his more prestigious—or intellectually more fashionable—contemporaries is their consummate theatricality. Time and time again, and in plays of very varied tone and idiom, he has proved that he has a remarkable grasp of what works in theatrical terms. It would perhaps be too speculative to term such a feeling 'instinctive'; what is certain is that Anouilh's early penchant for the theatre was fostered and developed by a period spent as a young man as secretary to Louis Jouvet, and that throughout his half-century as a practising playwright he has had the closest possible relationship with his directors (he has in fact directed a number of plays himself), designers and actors. Moreover, whilst his is not a 'theatre of ideas' in the sense in which this term can obviously be applied to the philosophically motivated works of

Sartre or Camus on the one hand, and on the other to the more oblique, but equally pronounced, intellectualism of a Beckett, it is a theatre in which ideas are handled in a creative, thought-provoking manner. To avoid ambiguity, it might perhaps be more appropriate to apply to it a label such as the 'theatre of values' that has been proposed for the work of Molière.

In the middle of his career in the mid-1950s, Anouilh was to be profoundly influenced by Molière; but in his earlier years, he was receptive to a number of varied influences: the 'well-made play' of the commercial *théâtre des boulevards*; the poetic fantasy of Giraudoux; the surrealist imagination of Vitrac's *Victor, or Les Enfants au pouvoir*. Throughout his career, he has been a thoroughly traditional playwright: if he has been ready to experiment in the structure of his plays, and to use such devices as the play within the play or the cinematic flashback in a creative and inventive manner, in his attitude towards characters and dialogue he has always respected traditional concepts of coherence and causality. So that if his *pièces roses* like *Le Bal des voleurs* or *Léocadia* demonstrate a highly developed sense of the absurd, he has always eschewed the arbitrary and inconsequential techniques of 'Absurdist' theatre.

Incongruous though such a comparison may appear at first sight, Anouilh's career, and his peculiar quality as a playwright, present striking affinities with those of Pierre Corneille. In both cases we have a long active career, spanning half a century of production in various genres and dramatic modes: comedy, tragicomedy and tragedy on Corneille's part, matched by 'pièces roses' and 'pièces noires', followed by 'pièces brillantes', 'pièces grinçantes' and other hybrids in the case of Anouilh. With both dramatists, the whole *oeuvre* provides a fascinating framework, the study of which throws a valuable light on the evolution of characteristic attitudes as they recur in play after play; and most important, the nature of these attitudes, and the conflicts to which they give rise, reveal similar preoccupations on the part of the seventeenth-century and the twentieth-century playwrights. Just as the clash between 'l'éthique de la gloire' and the less exacting requirements of more worldly values provides the motive force of Corneille's heroic tragedy, so a similar conflict between intransigent idealism and more pragmatic values based on selfishness and materialism produces the dramatic action in a whole series of Anouilh's plays: H. G. McIntyre comments that 'there is only one central theme running through the whole of Anouilh's work—the eternal and universal conflict between idealism and reality' (p. 130). Moreover, with Anouilh as with Corneille, the idealism which inspires his characters is an arbitrary attitude, based not on any transcendental faith but on a subjective impulse; while, not unlike Corneille again, Anouilh showed an early aptitude for self-parody, deflating the themes treated with such serious intensity in his *pièces noires*, in the parallel series of *pièces roses*.

If, as has been suggested, each of Anouilh's plays gains a great deal from being considered in the context of his whole *oeuvre*, this is particularly the case with his later plays; and perhaps one relative weakness of his production from about 1960 onwards is that there seems to be no single play which can be sure of standing successfully on its own feet as a masterpiece. Among earlier works, however, there are a number which do measure up to that criterion, by virtue of the successful blend of characteristic theme with novel theatrical presentation. Among the *pièces roses* and *pièces brillantes*, *Le Bal des voleurs* and *L'Invitation au château* undoubtedly come into this category; so do *L'Alouette* and *Becket*, with their idiosyncratic treatment of historical subjects; and so, above all, does *Antigone*.

Performed for the first time in February 1944, *Antigone* invites comparison with Sartre's play *Les Mouches*, produced in June 1943. These two plays are the outstanding examples of the success of serious drama in Paris during the German occupation: a period when the theatre flourished as never before and when the theatregoing public, although looking for escapist subject-matter that would distract them from the grim realities of the contemporary situation, nevertheless sought intellectual stimulus, not mere ephemeral entertainment.

Subjects drawn from the mythology of the ancient world lent themselves admirably to this purpose. They offered the cultured spectator an original adaptation, or reinterpretation, of a classical theme; and the very nature of myth itself provided dramatists with the opportunity to make an indirect comment on the modern world by means of characters and relationships not tied down to a precise context of time or place.

After serving, together with ancient history, as one of the principal sources of subject-matter for the authors of neo-classical tragedy in the seventeenth and eighteenth centuries, the myths of the ancient world had been largely neglected by nineteenth-century playwrights in France, except for the highly entertaining burlesque parodies written by Meilhac and Halévy for Offenbach's operettas *Orphée aux enfers* and *La Belle Hélène*. The twentieth century, however, was to witness a brilliant revival of serious drama based on Greek myths, by writers either inspired by the search for theatricality and 'la poésie du théâtre', or else looking for a vehicle for philosophical ideas: a revival of interest in mythological material that has had no counterpart in the dramatic literature of any other European country.

André Gide led the way with his *Le Roi Candaule* (1901); and his treatment of the Oedipus theme (*Oedipe*, 1930) was to be followed most notably by those of Cocteau (*La Machine infernale*, 1934) and Ghéon (*Oedipe*, 1942). In the same period, Giraudoux produced his *Amphitryon 38* (1929), *La Guerre de Troie n'aura pas lieu* (1935) and *Électre* (1937); and Sartre too was to turn to the theme of Orestes and Electra during the 1939–45 war as the subject for

Les Mouches. But whereas Giraudoux's choice of mythological themes, like Cocteau's, was governed by a poet's creative vision, so that both these dramatists appeal to our imaginative, rather than to our intellectual, faculties —this is true even of plays like *Amphitryon 38* and *La Guerre de Troie*, in which a clear humanist message comes across in simple human terms—Sartre was to adopt the *Oresteia* theme for a more overtly didactic purpose; and of all these plays based on Greek myth, *Les Mouches* is the one in which characters are the most completely identified with the intellectual abstractions they represent. Whereas other dramatists have handled myth suggestively, allowing each reader or spectator to supply the reading that best fits in with his own subjective response, it is generally agreed that Sartre's manner leaves much less latitude for individual interpretation. Sartre's Oreste represents the enlightened mind, emancipated from dependence on superstition and the passive acceptance of tyranny; Égisthe, the tyrant whose rule requires the unquestioning obedience of his subjects and cannot survive a confrontation with the spirit of intellectual freedom. Not only does the theme of *Les Mouches* express ideas on freedom of choice which were of paramount importance to Sartre as a philosopher throughout his life; but the application to the political situation under the Occupation seems to us so unambiguous that it is difficult to understand that the play should have been tolerated by the German censorship.

In the case of *Antigone*, insofar as Anouilh's play expresses a comment on the contemporary situation, that comment certainly does not take the form of such a clear-cut message; and as regards the motives of a less topical nature that inspired its writing, these reflect, in place of Sartre's philosophical preoccupations, the aesthetic interests of a man of the theatre. For Anouilh's contemporaries, the immediate context was such that it inevitably took priority over other considerations; and the play was almost always seen as a political allegory by its first audiences. To readers and spectators forty years on, however, it must be doubtful whether this was ever Anouilh's dominant motivation; and with the advantage of hindsight, it seems more relevant to examine the links with the playwright's earlier works.

II *Anouilh's Theatre before* Antigone

Antigone was the second of Anouilh's plays to make use of a subject from classical mythology. The first had been *Eurydice*, in 1941, but this time he went further, and attempted a close adaptation of one of the best known of the surviving Greek tragedies, Sophocles' *Antigone*. However, both in *Eurydice* and in *Antigone* he reproduced themes that had recurred with obsessive frequency throughout his own serious theatre from the early 1930s onwards. The most interesting of these early plays in this respect is *La Sauvage*. Written in 1934 and performed in 1938, it expresses similar attitudes to those found in *L'Hermine* (1931) and *Jézabel* (1932); but with its greater theatrical impact, and offering as it does more scope for interpretative participation on the spectator's part, it stands out as the one serious play from this period of apprenticeship that anticipates a masterpiece like *Antigone* not only in its theme but in its technique as well.

One important link between *La Sauvage* and *Antigone* is the entirely subjective nature of the heroine's motivation in both plays. Franz, the hero of *L'Hermine*, had committed murder in order to achieve his ambition of material ease and happiness with Monime, whom he loves: an immoral act, but one which is explainable according to the logic of cause and effect. Marc, in *Jézabel*, had rejected the possibility of happiness with his fiancée Jacqueline, on the discovery of his mother's criminality: an action more in keeping with moral principles, and again understandable in terms of normal causality. In *La Sauvage*, however, the behaviour of Thérèse, the heroine, is much less amenable to rational explanation. She too has a chance to escape from the sordid vulgarity of her family background—her parents play (like Anouilh's own mother) in a third-rate cafe orchestra—by marrying Florent, a rich and talented musician. When she finally turns her back on the promise of a happy marriage to Florent, and reverts to the familiar squalor of life with her parents, this may seem like an echo of Marc's renunciation of happiness with Jacqueline; but conventional moral scruples play little part in Thérèse's decision. This is the product of instinctive, irrational forces within her; and her cry:

> Vous me dégoûtez tous avec votre bonheur! On dirait qu'il n'y a que le bonheur sur la terre. Hé bien, oui, moi, je ne veux pas me laisser prendre par lui toute vivante. Je veux continuer à avoir mal et à souffrir, à crier, moi! C'est extraordinaire, n'est-ce pas? Vous ne pouvez pas comprendre, n'est-ce pas?

reveals a fundamental opposition, between those who are content to accept life as it is, with its concessions and its compromises, and the intransigent idealists who refuse to compromise with their absolute values: values which are in the final analysis, like the 'éthique de la gloire' which animates Corneille's heroes, aesthetic rather than moral in character. One element, certainly, in the case of Thérèse, is a feeling of solidarity with the underprivileged:

Tu comprends, Florent, j'aurai beau tricher et fermer les yeux de toutes mes forces . . . Il y aura toujours un chien perdu quelque part qui m'empêchera d'être heureuse. (Act III)

However, her affinity with other Anouilh characters, whose behaviour shows no evidence of such moral impulsion, betrays the fundamental illogicality of their motivation. Monsieur Henri, the omniscient 'meneur du jeu' of *Eurydice*, says to Orphée in a much-quoted passage:

— Mon cher, il y a deux races d'êtres. Une race nombreuse, féconde, heureuse, une grosse pâte à pétrir, qui mange son saucisson, fait ses enfants, pousse ses outils, compte ses sous, bon an mal an, malgré les épidémies et les guerres, jusqu'à la limite d'âge; des gens pour vivre, des gens pour tous les jours, des gens qu'on n'imagine pas morts. Et puis il y a les autres, les nobles, les héros. Ceux qu'on imagine très bien étendus, pâles, un trou rouge dans la tête, une minute triomphants avec une garde d'honneur ou entre deux gendarmes selon: le gratin. Cela ne vous a jamais tenté?
— Jamais, et ce soir moins que jamais.
— C'est dommage. Il ne faut pas croire exagérément au bonheur. Surtout quand on est de la bonne race. On ne se ménage que des déceptions. (Act II)

The tragic fatalism that he evokes merely makes more explicit what had been implied in *La Sauvage* (and even in *L'Hermine* and *Jézabel*), and what was to be present as a potent motive force in the whole of Anouilh's serious theatre up to the middle 1950s: the predestined role of an élite, living on a higher plane of sensibility than those around them, and fated to suffer because of the incompatibility of their ideals with the requirements of ordinary everyday living.

In *Eurydice*, we have a highly imaginative transposition of the original Greek myth into the contemporary world with which we are already familiar from Anouilh's other early plays. Orphée is an itinerant musician, accompanying his pathetic failure of a father from one precarious engagement to another; Eurydice is a member of a travelling dramatic troupe, accompanying her grotesquely overbearing mother and subject to sexual blackmail from the director of the company. The couple meet at a railway station between trains; and their short-lived idyll begins. From the start, there is a discrepancy between the idealized picture of Eurydice in Orphée's mind, and what we see of Eurydice herself; and when Eurydice is returned from the dead, by the good offices of Monsieur Henri, Orphée loses her again by disobeying the latter's instructions and looking at her—not (as in the original form of the myth) because of his fear of losing her, but because he needs to convince himself that she is telling the truth. Here, the relationship between the legendary Orpheus and Eurydice serves as a fruitful metaphor, enhancing the dramatic effect of the relationship between their twentieth-century counterparts. Nowhere is this metaphor more suggestive than at the end of Act I, where the young couple, wholly absorbed in each other, have abandoned their respective parents and are prepared to start a new life together:

> — Mon amour.
> — Mon cher amour.
> — Voilà l'histoire qui commence . . .
> — J'ai un peu peur . . . Es-tu bon? Es-tu méchant? Comment t'appelles-tu?
> — Orphée. Et toi?
> — Eurydice.

Anouilh was to make a similar use of metaphor in his *Roméo et Jeannette* (1945), another play in a contemporary setting, in which the reference to Shakespeare's tragedy, though it is never made explicit, is ever-present, and gives an extra dimension to the imaginative content of the drama. But in *Antigone*—and the same is true of *Médée* (1946)—the relationship between the original myth and the playwright's adaptation of it works in a different way. For Sophocles' version does not act as mere metaphorical reference or poetical embellishment: it provides not the sub-text, but the text itself; and instead of an action set in our own day, given an extra dimension by allusive evocation of ancient myth or Shakespearean tragedy, Anouilh offers us an action set in ancient Thebes, with life in the twentieth century providing the metaphorical enrichment. Compared with the other outstanding adaptations of Greek myth in the modern French theatre, Cocteau's *La Machine infernale*, Giraudoux's *Électre* and Sartre's *Les Mouches*, Anouilh's play is by far the closest to its Sophoclean original. What has Sophocles' *Antigone* to offer to a modern playwright, and why should Anouilh have been attracted to the subject at this stage of his career?

III *From Sophocles to Anouilh: the Oedipus and Antigone Theme*

The legend of the house of Thebes has survived in part in Aeschylus' *Seven against Thebes* and in Euripides' *Phoenissae*; and in a remarkably full treatment in Sophocles' sequence of plays *Oedipus Rex*, *Oedipus at Colonus* and *Antigone*[1]. It is not possible fully to understand the subject-matter of the *Antigone* (or of the modern derivatives of Sophocles' play) without a knowledge of the earlier part of the legend, as recorded in the first two plays of the sequence.

The essence of the legend is as follows. King Laius of Thebes and his Queen Jocasta have been told by an oracle, before the birth of their son, that the child will grow up to kill his father and marry his mother. To forestall this sinister prediction, though they are unwilling actually to put their own child to death, they send a faithful servant to expose him on Mount Cithaeron, his feet pierced by an iron pin. The servant, unable to bring himself to leave the infant to die, hands him over to a shepherd of Corinth who is grazing his flocks on the mountain, to bring up as his own son. However, the King of Corinth, Polybus, and his wife Merope are childless, and they gladly adopt the child, naming him Oedipus, or Swollen-foot, because of the injury inflicted on him. Oedipus grows up as the son of Polybus and Merope, until in due course he in his turn hears the same prediction from the oracle of Apollo: that he will kill his father and marry his mother. He resolves to defeat the oracle by leaving Corinth and never seeing his supposed parents again. He travels, and after a contretemps at a crossroads at Daulis—an impatient old man disputes the right of way, provokes a quarrel, and is killed by Oedipus in the ensuing fight—he arrives at Thebes. There, he saves the kingdom from the oppression of the Sphinx by guessing her riddle, enters the city in triumph to claim the hand of the Queen, who has just been widowed. . . .

The action of *Oedipus Rex* takes place after fifteen years of happiness and prosperity, during which Jocasta has borne Oedipus two sons and two daughters. The gods have now inflicted a plague on the city, and when the oracle at Delphi is consulted, it announces that this is because the murderer of Laius has gone unpunished. Oedipus, the wise and successful King, bends all his energy to finding the man responsible, and to saving his fellow-citizens. One by one, the clues are pieced together. Jocasta, perceiving the awful truth before her husband, hangs herself; when Oedipus in his turn is enlightened, he blinds himself in horror. Creon, Jocasta's brother, takes control of the kingdom, and Oedipus goes into exile with his young daughter Antigone.

In the second play, the exiled King and his faithful daughter have come to a final resting-place on holy ground at Colonus, near Athens, whose King, Theseus, offers sanctuary, and is willing to protect his guest both against Creon and against Oedipus's own son Polynices, who is about to lead the forces of Argos against his brother Eteocles, now King of Thebes. These two threats countered, Oedipus prepares himself for death; and the play closes with the moving narrative of his mysterious and enigmatic passing from this world.

Sophocles' *Antigone* opens at the point at which Oedipus's curse on his dis-loyal, belligerent sons has borne fruit: the invasion of Thebes has taken place, and Eteocles and Polynices have killed each other in single combat. Creon, now ruler again, decrees that Eteocles shall be buried with honour, but that the body of Polynices shall remain unburied, as a grim warning to other would-be traitors; and further, that any infringement of this decree shall incur the death penalty. Though her sister Ismene refuses to help her, Antigone defies Creon's order and covers her brother's body with earth; and in a scene of confrontation between the two characters she maintains her defiance, knowing it will cost her her life. Creon maintains his authoritarian order even though Haemon, his son, who is betrothed to Antigone, pleads with him to change his mind. However, when the blind seer Tiresias prophesies divine retribution, Creon decides to give burial to Polynices' remains, and to release Antigone from the tomb where she has been walled up alive. But this comes too late: Antigone has hanged herself in her tomb, and Haemon kills himself on her body. Queen Eurydice takes her own life on learning of her son's death, and Creon is left to bear the burden of his guilt.

It is the first episode of the legend, the disclosure of Oedipus's identity as unwitting parricide, and son and husband to Jocasta, that has attracted most modern playwrights: Gide, for instance, because it gave him the chance to explore, as Corneille (1659) and Voltaire (1718) had done in their versions, the problem of human responsibility in a world in which men are denied free will; Ghéon, as a Catholic writer, who gave an idiosyncratic twist to the myth as the working-out of original sin on the part of Oedipus's parents; and Cocteau, a distinctive feature of whose version is that it introduces a Freudian interpretation of the relationship between Oedipus and Jocasta. A number of playwrights—Garnier in his *Antigone* (1580)[2] as well as Rotrou in his play of the same name (1639); and Racine in *La Thébaïde* (1664), like the Italian Alfieri (*Polinice*, 1783)—had all chosen to dramatize that part of the legend which falls between the *Oedipus at Colonus* and the *Antigone* (and which is recorded in Aeschylus' and Euripides' extant plays on the subject): the fatal rivalry between the two brothers, enemies from birth; in these versions Antigone has a central, though a passive, role, as an anguished spectator, powerless to prevent the mutual destruction of her brothers. Anouilh, on the other hand, restricted himself to the final stage of the myth, after the death of Eteocles and Polynices, a stage which centres not on man's persecution by the gods, or an alien destiny (Cocteau's title provides an explicit reference to the 'mechanical' means by which, according to his interpretation, the gods ensure the destruction of their victim), but on the conflict between the human will and human authority.

Partly, no doubt, this was because of the ideological possibilities inherent in a topical application of the subject; but a more cogent reason, surely, was the affinity between Antigone the rebel, the individualist, and the typical heroes and heroines of previous plays. It is obviously not due to any oversight that Antigone's speech in her central scene with Créon:

> Vous me dégoûtez tous avec votre bonheur! Avec votre vie qu'il faut aimer coûte que coûte. On dirait des chiens qui lèchent tout ce qu'ils trouvent. Et cette petite chance, pour tous les jours si on n'est pas trop exigeant. Moi, je veux toùt, tout de suite,—et que ce soit entier,—ou alors je refuse! Je ne veux pas être modeste, moi, et me contenter d'un petit morceau si j'ai été bien sage. Je veux être sûre de tout aujour d'hui et que cela soit aussi beau que quand j'étais petite—ou mourir

should repeat a phrase we have already quoted from *La Sauvage*. A looser kind of self-quotation, in the form of repetition of attitudes and gestures, is by no means uncommon in Anouilh; but literal repetition of an expression used by an earlier character is sufficiently rare for us to be sure that this represents a deliberate indication of a 'family relationship' between the playwright's two heroines—a relationship which we may assume also to have included the heroine of Sophocles' play as Anouilh saw her.

On the other hand, it is interesting that the choice of the *Antigone* as model should apparently have led Anouilh to produce, in his own *Antigone*, a play in which the confrontation between the individual and the values of the state, or society, is a good deal more ambiguous, in terms of intellectual approval and emotional sympathy, than it had been in his previous plays. Evidence of this ambiguity is to be seen in the fact that contemporary comment was far from unanimous in seeing Antigone as the heroine of a play intended to rally support for the French Resistance; and that many of the first spectators and readers of *Antigone* accused Anouilh of supporting collaborationist activities by his sympathetic portrayal of Créon. Was such ambiguity the result of a deliberate attempt to cover his tracks, as George Steiner seems to suggest: 'Anouilh had to produce the work in the face of the enemy; he presented an *Antigone* at the court of Creon' (p. 330)? Was it an interpretation dictated by the stage he had reached in his own intellectual and artistic evolution? Or was it something deriving from a sympathetic understanding of the Greek original?

It is interesting to note in this connection that another modern French playwright, Albert Camus, was to pinpoint the concept of ambiguity as the distinguishing characteristic of all tragic drama. Adopting a principle formulated by the German philosopher Hegel in the nineteenth century, Camus writes:

> Sans prétendre trancher un problème devant lequel tant d'intelligences hésitent on peut, au moins, procéder par comparaison et essayer de voir en quoi, par exemple, la tragédie diffère du drame ou du mélodrame. Voici quelle me paraît être la différence: les forces qui s'affrontent dans la tragédie sont également légitimes, également armées en raison. Dans le mélodrame ou le drame au contraire, l'une seulement est légitime. Autrement dit, la tragédie est ambiguë, le drame simpliste. Dans la première, chaque force est en même

ambiguity

temps bonne et mauvaise. Dans le second, l'une est le bien, l'autre le mal (et c'est pourquoi de nos jours le théâtre de propagande n'est rien d'autre que la résurrection du mélodrame). Antigone a raison, mais Créon n'a pas tort . . . La formule du mélodrame serait en somme: 'Un seul est juste et justifiable' et la formule tragique par excellence: 'Tous sont justifiables, personne n'est juste'[3].

This text is of capital importance; and although the *Antigone* cited here is presumably that of Sophocles, what Camus says surely applies with equal force to Anouilh's play.

IV   *Sophocles'* Antigone: *Themes and Characters*

At first sight there might appear to be no better illustration of what Camus says about tragedy in general than Sophocles' version of the Antigone story. E. F. Watling writes:

> In *Antigone* . . . we are concerned with a single, and comparatively simple, conflict. A king, in full and sincere consciousness of his responsibility for the integrity of the state, has, for an example against treason, made an order of ruthless punishment upon a traitor and a rebel—an order denying the barest rites of sepulture to his body, and therefore of solace to his soul. A woman, for whom political expediency takes second place, by a long way, to compassion and piety, has defied the order and is condemned to death. Here is conflict enough, and tragedy—not in the martyrdom of obvious right under obvious wrong, but in the far more bitter, and at the same time exhilarating, contest between two passionately held principles of right, each partly justifiable, and each to a degree (though one more than the other) vitiated by stubborn blindness to the merits of the opposite. . . . (p. 13)

On the other hand, the parenthesis 'though one more than the other' makes a very important concession—so much so as to cast doubt on the balance between two 'principles of right'. A. J. A. Waldock makes the point effectively:

> In the *Antigone* there seems at first sight a genuine clash. One could not have a clearer grouping of parties, and the personal contest does appear this time to spring from an authentic collision of values. Divine law set against human law, family as opposed to state; whatever the precise phrasing one chooses, there would seem at first sight little doubt that in this case two high human principles compete. Yet even here is there real equivalence of powers? It is to be observed that the play itself has an answer—develops its own view of the

> question. After sundry false starts and hesitations the feeling of all who matter in the play swings unmistakably against Creon. . . . Everyone who counts is for Antigone; everyone who counts, against Creon. There is only one inference from this: the value represented by Creon is suspect. (pp. 30–1)

The psychological motivation of Sophocles' heroine has long been the subject of academic debate, though the precise nuances may not be of primary concern to us here. It may be her 'piety' that urges her to fulfil the burial rites out of a regard for the welfare of her brother's soul (since Greek religion taught that the souls of the unburied would never find rest); or it may be that, as H. D. F. Kitto claims, her defiant attitude depends on something less spiritual in nature, a strongly felt sense of human dignity:

> One has only to read the play to see that it contains not a single word about the peace of Polynices' soul. . . . What Sophocles emphasizes, time after time, is the mangling of Polynices' body. . . . What Sophocles relies on and presents again and again is the sheer physical horror, the sense of indecent outrage, that we all feel, modern English as well as ancient Greek, at the idea that a human body, the body of someone that we have known and maybe loved, should be treated like this. (pp. 148–9)

In either case, the reason for Antigone's rebellious act is less important than the act itself; though it is perhaps relevant to remark that to the extent that Kitto is right, to that extent Anouilh's heroine will prove to be the closer in her motivation to her Greek counterpart.

But if religious beliefs and religious practices arguably do not provide the key to Antigone's behaviour in this way, the religious dimension to the plot of Sophocles' play is nevertheless quite unmistakable. As more than one commentator has suggested, the gods operate through Antigone, but their hidden purpose has more to do with Creon than with the eponymous heroine herself. Looked at as a play about Antigone, Sophocles' tragedy must indeed appear distinctly lacking in balance. Antigone goes out to her death at line 807 (of a total of 1176 lines)[4]; at the end of the play, when Tiresias' prophecy has been fulfilled and Haemon has killed himself over the dead body of his beloved, one body alone is carried in to confront Creon with the consequences of his obstinate folly: that of his son; and there is not even a single reference to Antigone during the last 90 lines. The structure of Sophocles' *Antigone* is based, not on a duel between two characters, but on a triangular relationship—Antigone and Haemon do not meet, but the latter appears for a crucial scene with his father before the death-sentence on Antigone is irrevocably confirmed—and there can be no doubt that the principal focus is on Creon. Structurally, because he occupies the stage during the all-important closing scenes; and thematically, because he illustrates in his person the concepts, essential to the working-out of the tragic process, of *hamartia*, the tragic flaw, and *anagnorisis*, recognition or discovery. The form taken by the hero's tragic guilt in this play is that of a mistaken judgement—'tragic error' would be the best rendering of *hamartia* here—and in this the *Antigone* is not untypical of Sophocles' practice. As C. M. Bowra writes:

> The conflict in Sophoclean tragedy is mainly between divine and human purposes. It may, and usually does, involve conflicts between human beings, but in the last resort it arises from the differences between gods and men, from men's ignorance of their own state, or refusal to do what the gods demand.

'Antigone throughout acts for the gods, and in resisting her Creon resists them and pays for it', says Bowra in the same passage (p. 36). The theme of the Greek play, and the source of the tragedy, is therefore this: the gods watch over the preservation of a certain order in human affairs; men will offend against this divine order through their blindness and ignorance, and when they occupy positions of great power, their error will involve the destruction of others. The tragic effect is created by the pathos deriving from this destructive process, but more particularly by the awakening to awareness of responsibility and guilt on the part of the central character. In the *Antigone*, Tiresias acts as the conscious agent of the gods; such is his role when he appears at the end of the play, to set the dénouement in motion:

> Ere the chariot of the sun
> Has rounded once or twice his wheeling way,
> You shall have given a son of your own loins
> To death, in payment for death—two debts to pay:
> One for the life that you have sent to death,
> The life you have abominably entombed;
> One for the dead still lying above ground
> Unburied, unhonoured, unblest by the gods below.
> You cannot alter this. The gods themselves
> Cannot undo it. It follows of necessity
> From what you have done. Even now the avenging Furies,
> The hunters of Hell that follow and destroy,
> Are lying in wait for you, and will have their prey,
> When the evil you have worked for others falls on you. (lines 922–35)

The Chorus, however, plays a more equivocal role. While the gods 'speak through' the Chorus, its members, being ordinary, fallible human beings, are not always aware of the truths they express; and such passages are a characteristic vehicle for Sophoclean irony, as when the Chorus comments on the Sentry's report that some unknown person has disobeyed Creon's edict by scattering earth on Polynices' body:

> . . . Great honour is given
> And power to him who upholdeth his country's laws
>   And the justice of heaven.
>   But he that, too rashly daring, walks in sin
> In solitary pride to his life's end,
> At door of mine shall never enter in
>   To call me friend. (lines 311–17)

Kitto comments on this passage: 'The Chorus has in mind the unknown lawbreaker who has buried the body; *we* know that the words fit Creon, and no one else in the play. We therefore interpret this last stanza in a deeper sense . . .' (p. 157).

Sophocles' tragic focus, then, is firmly on Creon: his is the downfall—the 'passage from good to bad fortune'—which illustrates the characteristic pattern of tragedy, and his the 'discovery' which completes the tragic process. On the other hand, it is difficult not to feel that the principal focus of our emotional interest, let alone of our sympathy, is on Antigone herself; and the first half of the play is devoted to establishing that interest and sympathy. By its construction, the *Antigone* belongs to a group of tragedies—some by Sophocles, some by Euripides—to which the label 'diptych' has been applied, to indicate a distinct shift of focus during the course of the play. In a most illuminating chapter dealing with this structural feature, Waldock suggests a reason for what may seem to us an avoidable lack of balance:

> It is not modern sentiment, merely, that causes us to regret the early departure of Phaedra [the example is taken from Euripides' *Hippolytus*, but the argument would apply with equal force to the heroine of the *Antigone*]; her departure is to be regretted for the strictest dramatic reasons . . . [but] a Greek play is not able to cope with a set of three people who are at once so important and so closely involved as [Creon and Antigone and Haemon]. For she could hardly have remained in the drama except at the price of a strong triangular clash, and that is a price that Greek drama is not prepared to pay. Greek drama has a number of examples to show of the mildly triangular scene, but it never overcame its distaste for the full-blooded triangular clash. (pp. 59–60)

The Greek tragedians were of course never subject to anything like the codified 'rules', prescribed by seventeenth-century French theorists, whose source was erroneously ascribed to Aristotle's *Poetics*: neither the technical, or structural, requirement of the three unities of time, place and action nor that fourth, unwritten 'unity', that of tone, whose effect throughout the neo-classical period was to be so much more inhibiting, was acknowledged by the Greeks. Greek playwrights were therefore free to indulge in a variety of dramatic styles quite unknown to Racine and his successors, a variety that can be appreciated even by those modern readers who are forced to depend on a translated text. Indeed, English readers, attuned to the rich contrasts of style to be found in Shakespeare's dialogue, are likely to respond particularly favourably to this feature.

It can be illustrated in Sophocles' *Antigone* both in the Chorus, whose lyrical and philosophical passages make it possible, in the manner of the Shakespearean soliloquy, for the particular affairs of individuals to take on a general and universal import; and also in the homely realism and material detail which characterize the speech of the Sentry:

> My lord, if I am out of breath, it is not from haste.
> I have not been running. On the contrary, many a time
> I stopped to think and loitered on the way,
> Saying to myself 'Why hurry to your doom,
> Poor fool?' and then I said 'Hurry, you fool.
> If Creon hears this from another man,
> Your head's as good as off'. So here I am,
> As quick as my unwilling haste could bring me;
> In no great hurry, in fact. So now I am here . . .
> But I'll tell my story . . . though it may be nothing after all.
> (lines 185–94)

> There was no sign of a pick, no scratch of a shovel;
> The ground was hard and dry—no trace of a wheel;
> Whoever it was had left no clues behind him.
> When the sentry on the first watch showed it us,
> We were amazed. The corpse was covered from sight—
> Not with a proper grave—just a layer of earth—
> As it might be, the act of some pious passer-by.
> There were no tracks of an animal either, a dog
> Or anything that might have come and mauled the body.
> Of course we all started pitching in to each other,
> Accusing each other, and might have come to blows,
> With no one to stop us; for anyone might have done it,
> But it couldn't be proved against him, and all denied it. . . .
> (lines 210–22)

Such realism has been compared to the 'comic relief' of Shakespearean tragedy, of which the best-known example is no doubt the scene with the drunken Porter in Act II of *Macbeth*, which separates the murder of Duncan from its discovery and all that follows. This can properly be seen as a structural feature, and its purpose is defended by Dryden, for instance: 'A continued gravity keeps the spirit too much bent; we must refresh it sometimes, as we bait in a journey, that we may go on with greater ease'[5]. However, this is surely not the purpose of episodes like that of the

Sophoclean Sentry. The character is demonstrably more fully integrated into the scheme of the play; and this is well brought out by Kitto's comment:

> It is customary for us, and indeed quite natural, to call this man a comic, or at least a sub-comic character. He seems to provide something like Shakespearean comic relief . . . but we have to be extremely careful. He is certainly a 'natural', vividly drawn from life; but Sophocles' reason for so drawing him is not a Shakespearean delight that such characters exist, and a willingness to relieve the tragic tension for a moment by putting such a delightful person into his play. If we sit back in our seats enjoying this man, relishing his garrulity, taking the scene as a charming naturalistic thumbnail sketch, we run the risk of missing the whole point. For example, the detail about the dust is the very reverse of naturalism. . . . (pp. 152–3)

For as Kitto says, the passage is followed by the Chorus's exclamation to Creon:

> My lord, I fear—I feared it from the first—
> That this may prove to be an act of the gods. (lines 236–7)

What is important here, not as comic relief but as part of the total meaning of the play, is the fact that the common people—the Sentry and the Chorus —have a vague perception of the divine purpose long before light dawns on Creon himself: the episode thus makes an important contribution to the spiritual, or religious, dimension of the *Antigone*. 'We must remember', Kitto reminds us, 'that the Greek gods operate not in a dim religious light, but in broad daylight'. (p. 157)

Moreover, this passage is very relevant to our interpretation of Anouilh's play. To talk of the *spiritual* dimension of the French *Antigone* may appear to beg the question; and its moral and intellectual context is very different indeed from that of Sophoclean drama. However, the same question is none-theless pertinent: do such passages represent the intrusion of a gratuitious form of 'comic relief', or do the reactions of Anouilh's common people like-wise contribute in some way to the rounded portrayal the playwright wishes to create?

With these issues present before us: the nature of the tragic event in Sophocles' scheme of things; the balance between characters and the focusing of the spectator's interest; and the tonal homogeneity, or lack of it, in the Greek version—and if possible, with a reading, or re-reading, of the Greek *Antigone* fresh in our minds—let us now proceed to a detailed analysis of Anouilh's text[6].

V Anouilh's Antigone: *An Analytical Commentary*

Though longer than Sophocles' original, Anouilh's is not a long play, and structurally the two works are very similar. Like the Greek tragedy, Anouilh's *Antigone* is not divided into acts, and is written for continuous playing without interval. Moreover, it respects in large measure the Greek convention referred to above, according to which there were seldom more than two principal characters on stage together, and each scene, or episode, was normally a dialogue. Here, the only exceptions are brief linking scenes in which one or more of the Gardes, La Nourrice or Le Choeur, is temporarily present with two of the principal characters, and one isolated occasion on which Créon, Antigone, and Ismène together occupy the stage for no more than a page of dialogue—the counterpart of a similar *scène à trois* in Sophocles (lines 453–508). For the rest, the play is constructed on the Sophoclean pattern, with a succession of fairly short scenes bringing together either Antigone or Créon and one other character—and as a centrepiece the magnificent long scene between the two main characters themselves, which on its own constitutes well over a quarter of the whole play. Since there are no formal indications in the published text, it may be useful to begin by setting down a scheme of scene-divisions for easy reference. If we follow the established French practice of indicating a new scene with the entrance or exit of a character or characters, we arrive at the following picture[7]:

(i)	pages	39–41	Prologue
(ii)		42–6	Antigone, La Nourrice
(iii)		46	Antigone, Ismène, La Nourrice
(iv)		46–51	Antigone, Ismène
(v)		51–3	Antigone, La Nourrice
(vi)		53–7	Antigone, Hémon
(vii)		57–8	Antigone, Ismène
(viii)		58–62	Créon, Le Garde
(ix)		62–3	Le Choeur
(x)		63–5	Antigone, Les Gardes
(xi)		65–8	Antigone, Créon, Les Gardes
(xii)		68–85	Antigone, Créon
(xiii)		85–6	Antigone, Créon, Ismène
(xiv)		86–7	Créon, Le Choeur
(xv)		87–9	Créon, Hémon, Le Choeur
(xvi)		89	Créon, Le Choeur
(xvii)		89	Créon, Antigone, Les Gardes, Le Choeur
(xviii)		90–5	Antigone, Le Garde
(xix)		95–6	Le Messager, Le Choeur

| (xx) | 96–7 | Créon, Le Page, Le Choeur |
| (xxi) | 97–8 | Le Choeur |

It will be seen that on one side of the central confrontation nearly all the scenes involve Antigone: she is indeed absent for only one scene, between Créon and Le Garde; while on the other side Créon is on stage virtually the whole time, the only substantial exception being a scene between Le Garde and Antigone: evidence of a care for balanced composition which suggests a debt to the Sophoclean example.

The list of *Personnages*, if we compare it with the *dramatis personae* of the Greek play, hints straightaway both at the closeness of Anouilh's adaptation and at the nature of the changes he has introduced. The substitution of the Gardes (three speaking parts) for a single Sentry allows Anouilh to fill out, and embroider on, the dialogue reported in Sophocles (lines 219ff, 370ff); the Page de Créon is a functional character with a handful of lines, who exists purely as a recipient of the King's confidences, especially in the closing lines of the play. The principal characters—Créon, Antigone, Ismène, and Hémon, even Le Messager and Eurydice—are taken over (though Eurydice becomes a non-speaking part); and the only substantive changes appear to be that Tiresias is missing from the list, and that Antigone is provided with a *confidente* in the form of her old nurse. If the absence of the blind prophet suggests a 'désacralisation', or rationalization, of the mythical subject-matter, we can presume that the introduction of the Nourrice will act as a complement to this, and enable the French playwright to develop sympathy for his heroine on a more familiar domestic level.

There is one entry among the *dramatis personae* that is somewhat deceptive, however. 'Le Choeur' is by no means a simple equivalent of the Greek Chorus—which we may take, incidentally, to have been composed of the standard number of twelve or fifteen members, elders of the city of Thebes and therefore with a stake at first hand in the fortunes of its rulers. Anouilh's Choeur, or Prologue[8], on the other hand, is an individual, almost entirely detached from the action, and placed, as we shall see, in the unique position of privileged commentator, which suggests a loose comparison (inasmuch as he provides authorial comment) with the 'omniscient narrator' of prose fiction. In dramaturgical terms, the function of the Shakespearean Chorus (who speaks the Prologue to *Romeo and Juliet*, for instance, or the Prologue and Epilogue to *Henry V*) offers a closer analogy than the Chorus of Greek tragedy; though the role of Anouilh's Choeur is subtler and more idiosyncratic than this. In addition to his expository function (pp. 39–42, 62–3) and his function as Epilogue (pp. 97–8), this character does also on occasion assume the more traditional guise of confidant and mentor to Créon (pp. 86–9), and even acts as a supplementary messenger (pp. 95–6). Far from being a conventional figure, Le Choeur represents Anouilh's principal innovation; and our attitude towards this feature will play a large part in determining our critical interpretation of the play.

About the staging of the play there is only this to say: that Anouilh seems deliberately to have left this unspecified, and himself to have envisaged a 'décor neutre', or purely functional space, with a minimum of embellishment. The ideal, as regards both set and costume, is surely that both should be as unobtrusive as possible, leaving the whole emphasis (possibly assisted by lighting effects) squarely on the characters themselves. Photographs of the early Paris productions show a set of this nature: plain drapes, three steps leading up to a semicircular rostrum, and a pair of simple stools; while the costume (the men wear either evening dress or dinner-jackets; the guards black raincoats; and the women long black dresses except for Ismène who wears white) is similarly intended to leave the greatest possible freedom to the actors[9]. The photograph of the New York production of 1946, on the other hand, looks wrong: Cedric Hardwicke (Créon) and Katherine Cornell (Antigone), although dressed in a similar manner to their French counterparts, suggest a scene from a drawing-room comedy because the furniture and drapes convey an atmosphere, not of functional austerity but of elegance and comfort. Anouilh obviously had in mind an indoor set, but that is about as far as the decor ought to go: the designer should aim at something with the same non-committal character, *mutatis mutandis*, as the open-air Greek stage.

(i) Le Prologue (p. 39)

The curtain rises on the 'décor neutre', revealing all the characters on stage, who 'bavardent, tricotent, jouent aux cartes' during the long speech by the Prologue with which the play opens. The fact that they are all on stage to begin with, occupied in a variety of day-to-day activities, and that they get up and leave in turn towards the end of the Prologue's speech, to return only as and when the action requires their presence, brings convincing visual reinforcement to the idea implicit in what he says: that as well as being characters in Anouilh's play ('tous les *personnages* . . .'), these are members of a company of actors, waiting to assume the roles assigned to them in the forthcoming performance. In other words, Anouilh can be seen to be already suggesting an idea here that he will exploit more explicitly at the beginning of *L'Alouette* (1953), where the opening stage-direction reads in part:

> En entrant, les personnages décrochent leurs casques ou certains de leurs accessoires qui avaient été laissés sur scène à la fin de la précédente représentation, ils s'installent sur les bancs dont ils rectifient l'ordonnance. . .[10].

However, the Prologue does not say 'Ces acteurs vont vous jouer l'histoire d'Antigone', but 'Ces personnages . . .'. So that even when the actors have taken on their allotted parts within the play, they are still going to be performing, or acting out, a predetermined course of events: a notion that is at once given a most challenging illustration: 'Antigone . . .' (that is, not merely the actress playing the part, but the created character within the play) '. . . pense qu'elle va être Antigone tout à l'heure'. For the time being, she is 'la petite maigre . . . assise là-bas', 'la maigre jeune fille noiraude et renfermée . . .'; but her destiny, of which she is aware, is already calling her to make her stand against Créon, and to die for it. She is set apart from us, the spectators, 'qui sommes là bien tranquilles à la regarder, . . . qui n'avons pas à mourir ce soir'—set apart not only because as an actress she has stepped into the imaginary world on the other side of the footlights, but also because in her role as Antigone she is marked by a tragic destiny that does not concern itself with ordinary men and women.

It is easy to become over-familiar with a well known text, with the result that one may come to overlook its challenging or provocative character. This opening paragraph is a remarkable *tour de force*, presenting as it does with such economy of language the striking interplay of different levels of reality and illusion, and introducing the notion of life as the acting out of preordained roles, which will figure prominently in later scenes.

Ismène is contrasted throughout with Antigone, in every possible way. It is a contrast that could no doubt be said to be implicit in Sophocles, but from the beginning Anouilh makes it explicit: 'la blonde, la belle, l'heureuse Ismène' establishes her as the opposite of 'la maigre jeune fille noiraude et renfermée . . .' with her 'petit sourire triste'. The anecdotal account of the betrothal of Antigone and Hémon again develops suggestions that are perhaps latent in the Greek text, though in this case more of Anouilh's own gratuitous invention has gone into it. In particular, the effect of the anecdote is to present the relationship in anachronistic terms: though much less glaring than some of the examples that are to follow, the deliberate anachronism of 'un soir de bal où il n'avait dansé qu'avec Ismène', 'éblouissante dans sa nouvelle robe', 'L'orchestre attaquait une nouvelle danse', 'Ismène riait aux éclats . . . au milieu des autres garçons' is an attempt to close the gap between the mythological figures and the members of a twentieth-century audience. The last sentence of this paragraph: 'Il ne savait pas qu'il ne devait pas exister de mari d'Antigone . . .' reverts to the suggestive fatalism of the opening lines, and with 'ce titre princier . . .' the language takes on a more elevated tone; but the overall effect of the paragraph is to make the spectator feel: 'these are characters like ourselves'; they are no longer the remote heroes of a centuries-old tradition.

The thumbnail sketch of Créon looks forward to what will be the dominant traits of Anouilh's King: 'Il a des rides, il est fatigué. Il joue au jeu

difficile de conduire les hommes'. Again, suggestive touches bridge the gap
and help us to envisage Créon in twentieth-century terms, not only as a man
of culture and a patron of the arts: 'la musique, les belles reliures, les longues
flâneries chez les petits antiquaires de Thèbes', but also as a man of conscience
devoted to his duty: 'il a retroussé ses manches . . .', '. . . comme un ouvrier
au seuil de sa journée'.

Eurydice, with her knitting, is an Anouilh stereotype: compare La Mère in
L'Alouette, who similarly 'tricotera pendant toute la pièce, sauf quand c'est à
elle'; and so are the card-playing Gardes. 'Ils sentent l'ail, le cuir et le vin
rouge . . .': here Anouilh is using his Prologue very much like an omniscient
novelist, for 'Ils sentent . . .' is not something demonstrable, that spectators
can test empirically; we have to take the author's word for it, as an 'objective
correlative' of their mental limitations: '. . . et ils sont dépourvus de toute
imagination'.

The Prologue's last paragraph discreetly fulfils a traditional expository
function, with a brief summary of the antecedents of the plot: the events
following on the exile of Oedipus and the curse laid on his sons. The events,
indeed, of Racine's tragedy *La Thébaïde*; and Anouilh's phrase 'les deux
frères ennemis sont morts . . .' reproduces, no doubt intentionally, the
subtitle (*Les Frères ennemis*) of that play. At this point, the closing lines of the
Prologue's speech bring us into the closest contact yet with Sophocles' text,
where Antigone says:

> Eteocles has been buried, they tell me, in state,
> With all honourable observances due to the dead.
> But Polynices, just as unhappily fallen—the order
> Says he is not to be buried, not to be mourned;
> To be left unburied, unwept, a feast of flesh
> For keen-eyed carrion birds. (lines 20–5)

(ii) Antigone, La Nourrice (p. 42)

The dialogue begins with a passage of considerable charm, which owes
nothing to the Greek original. Antigone's poetic evocation of the distinctive beauty of the hour before dawn, with its personification of the sleep-
ing world of nature, has something in it of the imaginative quality of
Giraudoux's prose-poetry ('Le jardin dormait encore. Je l'ai surpris,
nourrice. Je l'ai vu sans qu'il s'en doute. C'est beau un jardin qui ne pense pas
encore aux hommes . . . je me suis glissée dans la campagne sans qu'elle s'en
aperçoive'), and one might be tempted to remember Anouilh's admiration
for that writer. However, this is not 'fine writing' for its own sake: the
poetic touches are entirely acceptable in their context, where they help to
characterize Antigone as herself a child of nature, and there is none of the

straining after effect that sometimes marks Giraudoux's 'preciosity'.

At various points during this scene the dialogue almost takes on a comic tone, as Antigone and the Nourrice talk at cross purposes; not only does Antigone deliberately play on her old nurse's misunderstanding of the situation, but the Nourrice, alternately solicitous and scolding, acts on the familiar level of ordinary domestic considerations ('Il va falloir te laver les pieds avant de te remettre au lit . . . Je me lève pour voir si elle n'était pas découverte. Je trouve son lit froid . . .'), while Antigone on the other hand constantly invests the ordinary with a mysterious significance. The conversation between these two characters is of course a complete innovation, and indeed their invented relationship is one of the factors that contribute to the 'rounding' of Antigone's personality, and help to establish her close affinity with other early Anouilh heroines. Not that the whole scene is equally successful in this respect: the fragment of imaginary dialogue between the Nourrice and the dead Jocasta is somewhat laboured, and borders on the sentimental ('Voilà ce qu'elle me dira, ta mère, là-haut, quand j'y monterai, et moi j'aurai honte, honte à en mourir si je n'étais pas déjà morte, et je ne pourrai que baisser la tête et répondre: "Madame Jocaste, c'est vrai" '); but it is obviously introduced in order to prepare the way for Antigone's cryptic hint: 'Elle sait pourquoi je suis sortie ce matin'. More hints, in which the fate-motif is adumbrated ('. . . je n'aurai jamais d'autre amoureux. . .', 'il ne faut pas que je sois petite ce matin') bring the scene to a close, as Ismène enters and the Nourrice departs to prepare an anachronistic cup of coffee.

(iii)–(iv) Antigone, Ismène, La Nourrice (p. 46)

From the beginning of this scene too, it is evident that the two speakers are not on the same 'wavelength'; but this time it is not so much a question of a 'sub-text'—mysterious hints that remain to be elucidated—as of an open and explicit difference of viewpoint. The subject of their disagreement is clear, since the Prologue has already informed us of Créon's edict; and throughout this scene we see disobedience, rebellion, contrasted with conformism and acceptance. Ismène's opposition to her sister is categorical: it is based on temperamental difference ('Tu es folle . . . Nous ne pouvons pas . . . Il nous ferait mourir . . . Je ne veux pas mourir'), and it is also backed up by rational argument: '. . . je comprends un peu notre oncle . . . Il est le roi, il faut qu'il donne l'exemple'. Antigone, for her part, is capable of expressing a wistful regret for what might have been ('Moi aussi j'aurais bien voulu ne pas mourir'); but she answers her sister in an equally categorical fashion, giving expression to the life-as-theatre metaphor which contributes so powerfully to the fatalistic theme of the play: 'A chacun son rôle. Lui, il doit nous faire mourir, et nous, nous devons aller enterrer notre frère. C'est comme cela que ç'a été distribué'.

On the other hand, it is clear from the beginning that Antigone's ready acceptance of this fate also depends on subjective, temperamental factors ('Moi je ne veux pas comprendre un peu . . . Je ne veux pas avoir raison . . .'). Her long speech: 'Comprendre . . . Vous n'avez que ce mot-là dans la bouche, tous, depuis que je suis toute petite . . .' may seem more suited, in some of its familiar detail ('Il fallait comprendre qu'on ne peut pas toucher à l'eau . . . Il fallait comprendre qu'on ne doit pas manger tout à la fois . . .'), to the situation of other Anouilh heroines than to that of a high-born daughter of the court of Thebes; but there can be no doubt that Anouilh's Antigone is presented as a consistent personality from the beginning, and the intransigent opposition to Créon is already being prepared in her stand against Ismène which, however arbitrary it may appear, unambiguously establishes her refusal to compromise: 'Comprendre. Toujours comprendre. Moi je ne veux pas comprendre. Je comprendrai quand je serai vieille . . .'.

The scene with Ismène also gives expression to the important paradox that this character who seemingly arbitrarily renounces the possibility of life and happiness, does so in the name of a love of life more intense than that of her sister:

> Qui se levait la première, le matin, rien que pour sentir l'air froid sur sa peau nue? Qui se couchait la dernière seulement quand elle n'en pouvait plus de fatigue, pour vivre encore un peu de la nuit? Qui pleurait déjà toute petite, en pensant qu'il y avait tant de petites bêtes, tant de brins d'herbe dans le pré et qu'on ne pouvait pas tous les prendre?

This speech develops the 'child of nature' theme of the opening scene, and establishes a positive complement to her apparent death-wish.

W. M. Landers, commenting on this scene in his edition of the play, writes as follows:

> Ismène's attitude here is quite different from that of her namesake . . . The Ismene of Sophocles hangs back through fear of the consequences; she confesses to a sense of guilt at not helping her sister and entreats the dead to forgive her. Anouilh's Ismène is really on Créon's side, at least in the early part of the play . . .

and also cites the 'shift in the attitude of the populace', who, according to Ismène, here side with Créon, as evidence of a desire to 'equalize the moral forces opposed to each other in the central scene' (p. 101). It seems rather that these are subsidiary considerations, and that fundamentally the French Ismène, like her Greek counterpart, is motivated by lack of courage, so that when she says 'Je comprends un peu notre oncle' and 'ils pensent tous comme lui dans la ville', she is trying to rationalize what is essentially a question of temperament. Her final plea: 'C'est bon pour les hommes de croire aux idées et de mourir pour elles. Toi tu es une fille' is not only a close verbal echo of Sophocles' text at this point:

> O think, Antigone; we are women; it is not for us
> To fight against men . . . (lines 52–3)

but it also expresses what I take to be the essence of the character's psychological motivation in both plays.

(v) Antigone, La Nourrice (p. 51)

The Nourrice's entry with coffee and *tartines* takes us away from Sophocles again; and in the theatre, this second scene of familiar dialogue on domestic matters has the effect of lowering the dramatic tension. The scene has been criticized for an excess of sentimentality: this is a matter of subjective taste, though it may well seem to most readers or spectators that Anouilh is taking something of a risk by placing such emphasis on the heroine's childlike relationship with her old nurse. The series of appellations 'mon pigeon', 'ma petite colombe', 'ma mésange', 'ma tourterelle' would not be out of place in a comedy; indeed, Anouilh uses a similar sequence elsewhere for comic effect.[11] On the other hand, Antigone's own affectionate appeal to the simple certainties of the past ('Mais fais-moi tout de même bien chaud comme lorsque j'étais malade . . .') is clearly meant to establish quite a different mood. But what might almost be seen as a kind of infantile regression on her part—suggested in the invocation of 'the wicked giant, the sandman, and the bogeyman who comes and steals little children away', together with the childlike rhythms of her speech at this point ('Alors je te le demande: ne la gronde pas. Promets que tu ne la gronderas pas. Je t'en prie, dis, je t'en prie, nounou . . . Et puis, promets-moi aussi que tu lui parleras, que tu lui parleras souvent') is surely rather overdone, and falls on the wrong side of the borderline between deeply-felt emotion and a more superficial sentiment. By the same token, the page devoted to the heroine's concern for the future of her dog, though it is no doubt intended to reinforce the feeling of foreboding that we by now share with Antigone, but which the Nourrice cannot share, runs the risk of producing the opposite effect by its build-up of homely detail, and of trivializing, rather than deepening, our relationship with the character.

(vi) Antigone, Hémon (p. 53)

The playwright is on surer ground in the scene between Antigone and Hémon: a scene that would have been out of place in Sophocles' version both for the structural reason discussed above, and also because his age took far less interest than we do in the literary possibilities of a romantic relationship between a pair of lovers. To have written a modern play on this subject, however, without taking the opportunity to bring the ill-starred lovers together, would have been virtually unthinkable; and as we have shown in our comments on the structure of Anouilh's play, above, the creation of this scene, which completes the triangular relationship between the principal characters, is one of the means by which the French dramatist produced a shift of emphasis, from the tragedy of Creon to a play whose focus is the conflict between Créon and Antigone. And while the subject-matter of the scene is of necessity just as new (and in fact may seem just as incongruous in relation to the Sophoclean material, for the notion of Antigone borrowing her sister's dress, perfume and lipstick in order to make herself attractive is another of the anachronisms that link her to characters like Thérèse and Jeannette), its effect is to heighten the emotional tension, and to increase our apprehension of impending catastrophe, rather than to dissipate them by means of irrelevance and triviality. Antigone's tender evocation of the child she and Hémon now will never have; her use of a conditional tense ('Le petit garçon que nous aurions eu . . . je l'aurais serré si fort . . . Il aurait eu une maman . . . plus sûre que toutes les mères . . . toi, tu aurais eu une vraie femme . . . j'aurais été très fière d'être ta femme . . .') that Hémon is unable to understand; her confession of an unsuccessful attempt to give herself to Hémon: all of these form part of a consistent build-up to the poignant climax of the scene, the elegiac ultimatum to her bewildered lover: '. . . jamais, jamais, je ne pourrai t'épouser' and the following speech, whose passionate intensity overcomes the threat of melodrama and carries complete conviction:

> Hémon, tu me l'as juré! Sors. Sors tout de suite sans rien dire. Si tu parles, si tu fais un seul pas vers moi, je me jette par cette fenêtre. Je te le jure, Hémon. Je te le jure sur la tête du petit garçon que nous avons eu tous les deux en rêve, du seul petit garçon que j'aurai jamais. Pars maintenant, pars vite. Tu sauras demain. Tu sauras tout à l'heure.

Hémon goes out at a high point of dramatic and emotional tension, all the more convincing because the scene has persuaded us of the couple's reciprocal affection. Hémon's is very much the more passive contribution, however, and it is Antigone who brings out the quality of their present relationship:

> Tu m'aimes, n'est-ce pas? Tu m'aimes comme une femme? Tes bras qui me serrent ne mentent pas . . .? Tes grandes mains posées sur mon dos ne mentent pas, ni ton odeur, ni ce bon chaud, ni cette grande confiance qui m'inonde quand j'ai la tête au creux de ton cou?

as well as the impossibility of a shared future, with her superlatives and temporal adverbs which stress the finality of the step she is taking: 'C'est la dernière folie . . . jamais, jamais, je ne pourrai t'épouser . . . [le] seul petit garçon que j'aurai jamais . . . C'est tout ce que tu peux faire encore pour moi . . .'.

Much has been written about the quality of love in the early Anouilh plays, where it frequently tends to take the form of a tender, loyal comradeship whose overtly sexual character is much played down: what H. Gignoux calls, in a happy phrase that is not too wide of the mark, 'une sorte de camaraderie garçonnière, de scoutisme mixte' (p. 71). Elsewhere, the images 'petit soldat', 'petit frère', 'petit copain' recur; and although Anouilh does not draw on the same range of imagery to portray the relationship between Antigone and Hémon, nevertheless there are certain clear hints of an affinity in this respect with the system of values in force in *La Sauvage* and *Eurydice*. When Antigone says: 'Je suis noire et maigre. Ismène est rose et dorée comme un fruit'; when she says: 'j'avais fait tout cela pour être un peu plus comme les autres filles'—even when she compares herself to other women with 'leurs vraies poitrines'—she is implicitly defending a conception of her relationship with Hémon that is based not on conventional ideas of sexual attraction, but on a comradeship that is essentially asexual. It is true that she confesses to having tried to lead Hémon on so that he might want her to give herself to him; but the fact that her attempt was frustrated perhaps indicates that she had been acting out of character. This in no way detracts from the intimacy of the couple; and indeed I think it adds to the emotive power of the situation. For the reader or spectator who can relate Antigone in this way to other early heroines of similar temperamental make-up, her gauche and inexpert attempt to achieve sexual fulfilment before she goes to her death gives an extra poignancy to the scene.

(vii) Antigone, Ismène (p. 57)

This brief scene is of capital importance: if not in terms of plot or character, at least in terms of dramatic impact. Ismène's second appearance represents another innovation—in Sophocles we see Ismene twice only, and her second scene corresponds to the French character's third appearance—and its justification is that it rounds off the exposition, properly speaking, and leads up to the tremendously effective 'curtain-line' that marks Antigone's exit: 'C'est trop tard. Ce matin, quand tu m'as rencontrée, j'en venais'. Preliminaries are now over, and the 'coup de théâtre' of this announcement brings us fully up to date with past events; if Anouilh had followed a conventional division into acts, this would have been the end of Act I. As it is, it is the first occasion on which the stage has been left empty between episodes, without what in neo-classical dramaturgy is called 'liaison des scènes'; and in the theatre, the director may well decide to emphasize the fact by a slightly longer pause before the next sequence begins.

(viii) Créon, Le Garde (p. 58)

Compared with Sophocles' Sentry, Anouilh's Garde is much more obviously a representative of the rough common soldier (cf. the stage-direction 'C'est une brute'); and despite the closeness in certain details to the Sophoclean text, there is a degree of caricatural exaggeration which suggests that Anouilh's aim here is much nearer to Shakespeare's: that is the creation of 'comic relief' for its own sake, rather than (as in Sophocles, if one can accept Kitto's comment, quoted above) the establishing of a coherent scheme of things in which the divine purpose finds expression in the most diverse kinds of humanity.

To begin with, it is the closeness to Sophocles that strikes one: the elements are the same, assembled flexibly and with a certain amount of discreet expansion:

> — It's this, sir. The corpse . . . someone has just
> Buried it and gone. Dry dust over the body
> They scattered, in the manner of holy ritual.
> — What! Who dared to do it?
> — I don't know, sir.
> There was no sign of a pick, no scratch of a shovel . . . (lines 205–18)[12]

> — Le cadavre, chef. Quelqu'un l'avait recouvert. Oh! pas grand' chose. Ils n'avaient pas eu le temps avec nous autres à côté. Seulement un peu de terre . . . Mais assez tout de même pour le cacher aux vautours.
> — Tu es sûr que ce n'est pas une bête en grattant?
> — Non, chef. On a d'abord espéré ça, nous aussi. Mais la terre était jetée sur lui, selon les rites. C'est quelqu'un qui savait ce qu'il faisait.
> — Qui a osé? Qui a été assez fou pour braver ma loi? As-tu relevé des traces?
> — Rien, chef. Rien qu'un pas plus léger qu'un passage d'oiseau . . .

The Greek guards, like the French, have drawn lots to see who shall carry the unwelcome message to Creon; and although Sophocles' Sentry is perhaps less prone than Anouilh's Garde to insinuate that his colleagues are more to blame than himself: 'On n'a pas parlé, chef, je vous le jure! Mais moi, j'étais ici et peut-être que les autres, ils l'ont déjà dit à la relève . . . ', there is a remarkable debt to the original, and this scene is in one sense one of the most closely copied in the whole play.

On the other hand, Anouilh's innovations and anachronisms are such as to give his Garde a distinct personality. With the mixture of servility and familiarity conveyed by the obtrusive 'chef' (which occurs no fewer than 21 times in this scene), the military jargon ('J'ai dix-sept ans de service. Je suis engagé volontaire, la médaille, deux citations. Je suis bien noté, chef. Moi je suis "service" . . .') and the popular expressions ('On est les trois du piquet de garde . . . Les autres c'est . . . Mes supérieurs ils disent . . .'), Garde Jonas, 'de la Deuxième Compagnie'[13], comes across as a coherent representation of a regular serving soldier in the modern idiom, as we know him from novels and films.

In Créon's case, the anachronisms are more discreet—'avec leur or bloqué dans Thèbes', for instance—so much so that it is possible to overlook even 'qui crachera devant mes fusils' at a first reading. But the whole of the long speech in which these phrases occur ('Un enfant . . . L'opposition brisée qui sourd et mine déjà partout . . .'), while not incompatible in general terms with the psychology of Sophocles' King, establishes Créon too as a sort of figure that is familiar to us in a modern context: a police chief or American state governor, perhaps—though 'les chefs de la plèbe puant l'ail' has a European rather than a transatlantic connotation. In this first meeting, Créon is presented as above all a realist. Not quite certain of the support of his people, suspicious of the role of the clergy, he is determined—unlike his Greek counterpart who insists on discovering the identity of the lawbreaker —to keep the matter quiet, so as not to provide a pretext for further unrest:

> . . . si tu parles, si le bruit court dans la ville qu'on a recouvert le cadavre de Polynice, vous mourrez tous les trois.

One of Anouilh's additions in this scene, unremarkable in itself, has a certain symbolic significance. This is the 'petite pelle d'enfant' (anachronistic in that we may assume that Oedipus and Jocasta were not in the habit of taking their young family for seaside holidays) which forms part of an important complex of references to childhood and the past—such as we have already commented on in the second scene with the Nourrice—by which the youth and the childlike qualities of Anouilh's heroine are established as a dominant motif. For the moment, the evidence of the spade serves to set Créon's suspicions on the wrong tack; but for the spectator who is already in the know, it symbolizes those values of incorruptible innocence and of obstinate determination to which Antigoné has already given expression. And as Créon goes out, the words he speaks to the young Page:

> Tu mourrais, toi, pour moi? Tu crois que tu irais avec ta petite pelle? . . .
> Oui, bien sûr, tu irais tout de suite toi aussi . . .

not only have the effect of showing a more humane, understanding aspect of his character, but can also be related in the spectator's mind to the theme of obstinate dedication to a cause on the part of Antigone herself.

(ix) Le Choeur (p. 62)

The reflections on tragedy by Le Choeur constitute one of the most distinctive and one of the best-known scenes of Anouilh's play. The practice of putting a mouthpiece of the author's on stage to express, not a comment on the specific action of the individual play, but generalizations about fate, free will or similar philosophical preoccupations is of course an extension of the practice of Greek tragedy, where choric odes commonly also departed from the play's specific context in order to utter philosophical truths of more general application, as in this example from the *Antigone* itself:

> Happy are they who know not the taste of evil.
> From a house that heaven hath shaken
> The curse departs not
> But falls upon all of the blood,
> Like the restless surge of the sea when the dark storm drives
> The black sand hurled from the deeps
> And the Thracian gales boom down
> On the echoing shore. (lines 509–16)

Among modern dramatists, Cocteau had most notably exploited the possibilities of this device. His own *Antigone* (1922) had virtually been an adaptation of Sophocles' text, somewhat abridged but little changed; but in a similar adaptation of Sophocles in *Oedipe-Roi* (1927) he had introduced a Prologue-chorus to comment on the cruelty of the gods in setting traps for men. This theme is developed, and given considerable prominence, in *La Machine infernale* seven years later; and Cocteau's dramaturgical invention here, as well as the specific image of the 'infernal machine' itself, must be considered as a major inspiration of the scene under consideration.

In Cocteau's play, the Prologue is used (as a disembodied Voice) not only to present the audience with a summary of the plot in advance, but also to comment on the action, which is described as follows:

> Regarde, spectateur, remonté à bloc, de telle sorte que le ressort se déroule avec lenteur tout le long d'une vie humaine, une des plus parfaites machines construites par les dieux infernaux pour l'anéantissement mathématique d'un mortel.

And at the beginning of each act, Cocteau uses La Voix to similar effect, in a manner more akin to that of the Shakespearean than of the Greek Chorus:

> La grande peste de Thèbes a l'air d'être le premier échec à cette fameuse chance d'Oedipe, car les dieux ont voulu, pour le fonctionnement de leur machine infernale, que toutes les malchances surgissent sous le déguisement de la chance . . . (Act IV)

From the beginning of this scene in Anouilh, the same metaphor recurs insistently ('Maintenant le ressort est bandé. Cela n'a plus qu'à se dérouler tout seul . . . on donne le petit coup de pouce pour que cela démarre . . . on n'a plus qu'à laisser faire . . . Cela roule tout seul. C'est minutieux, bien huilé depuis toujours'). This sustained image, borrowed from Cocteau, presents a similar, though not an identical, view of the tragic action—the difference being that according to Anouilh's Choeur the human victim seems to be involved in a mechanistic process (there is no indication as to who winds up the clockwork mechanism), whereas for Cocteau the process implies the hostility of the gods: supernatural beings who in his scheme of things have their own superior destiny which they must obey: 'Le mystère a ses mystères. Les dieux possèdent leurs dieux' (*La Machine infernale*, Act II). In human terms, however, the view of tragedy is essentially the same: it is an inexorable, impersonal process that man is powerless to resist.

The plot of *La Machine infernale* is fully consistent with that proposition and with its corollary, that free will does not exist. For whenever Oedipe thinks he is making a free choice in order to frustrate the oracle's prediction, he is in fact playing into the hands of fate and making his 'anéantissement' the more certain. But the application to Antigone's case is a good deal more ambiguous. It is true that the image of the tragic 'machine' fits in well enough with the life-as-theatre metaphor, the notion of the heroine acting out a pre-ordained destiny, which is expressed so challengingly in the opening lines spoken by Le Prologue; but as we shall see, this is not an interpretation to which we are necessarily led to subscribe by the main thrust of the action.

In the second paragraph of his soliloquy, Le Choeur sketches a contrast between tragedy and 'le drame' which prefigures, at least in its opening lines, the paragraph quoted above from Camus's 1955 lecture. 'Le drame' (that is to say, melodrama) is to do with the conflict between the wicked and the good ('ces traîtres'—the term always used of the 'villains' of melodrama— '. . . ces méchants acharnés . . . cette innocence persécutée'), whereas in tragedy 'On est tous innocents en somme'. This can be taken either to mean that, as Camus was to say—and as conventional theories of tragedy ever since Aristotle had claimed—the tragic hero is neither wholly good nor wholly bad, but a character of 'middling virtue'; or else perhaps to show that Anouilh is offering, as Landers suggests, a 'typically Romantic' view of 'Man as the eternal victim of creation' (p. 103). In any case, Le Choeur continues, 'C'est une question de distribution': all are acting out their predestined roles. And it is for this reason, no doubt, that tragedy is 'propre', 'reposant', 'tranquille'. Chance, the accidental and avoidable, are excluded from tragedy; there is no reprieve, no hope. This view of the tragic process has a long and reputable ancestry in the history of European literature— Landers suggests a parallel with the stoicism of Vigny's 'La Mort du loup', and there is also a clear affinity with the twentieth-century philosophy of the Absurd—but the resonance of 'le *sale* espoir' is peculiar to Anouilh, and to the very subjective scale of ethical values reflected in heroines like Thérèse and Antigone.

As Antigone enters, dragged in by the Gardes, Le Choeur's comment refers us back to the theme expressed in the opening lines of the play; while 'pour la première fois', together with 'pour la dernière fois' that we shall encounter later, provides a temporal framework for the unique tragic event, setting it apart from the accidental contingencies of ordinary everyday life.

(x) Antigone, Les Gardes (p. 63)

This brief linking scene creates the opportunity to develop the homely, popular element contributed to the play by the Gardes: the sort of lifelike vignette that Anouilh does so well. With their naive assumption that they are about to become national heroes, and their self-absorbed argument about the relative merits of eating-places, these are the simple soldiers of any modern army; but they are also representatives of a more timeless humanity. If their dialogue is comic, it is because of its unconscious incongruity in the present context. This may be the tragedy of the house of Thebes, but it is essential to Anouilh's purpose (as, less obviously, it had been to Sophocles') that the heroine's preoccupation with death be juxtaposed with the obtrusive continuity of ordinary life.

(xi) Antigone, Créon, Les Gardes (p. 65)

By contrast, the scene which follows returns us to Sophocles. The two supplementary guards now become non-speaking figures, and their spokes-man is given a narrative that closely corresponds to the original. Anouilh does not retain the feature ('a storm of dust, like a plague from heaven', line 358) which has suggested to some commentators a supernatural inter-vention, hiding Antigone's reappearance from the guards; and some other details are the result of analogical transposition rather than of translation. And similarly, the circumstantial detail with which Antigone herself invests the episode of the 'petite pelle' is obviously also an invention of the modern dramatist. For the rest, the narrative is handled with the same economy as in Sophocles, and the scene leads into, rather than holds up, the confrontation between the two central characters.

(xii) Antigone, Créon (p. 68)

Previous scenes have shown us that Créon is a realist, and that Antigone is pursuing some kind of ideal, or absolute; but the precise nature of their motives has not yet been revealed. It is the detailed unfolding of the characters' motivation, and the changing patterns of moral advantage—and therefore of sympathy in dramatic terms—that this produces, which provides the fascination of this justly celebrated scene. Not so much curiosity as to its outcome, for that we already know. We know Antigone is ordained to die, but not—in a play from which the gods are absent—how the moral forces, Camus's two 'forces légitimes', will be given dramatic expression.

Créon's first thought is to hush the matter up, and to prevent scandal ('tu vas rentrer chez toi . . . Je ferai disparaître ces trois hommes'); but Antigone firmly rejects this expedient, with the first of her reasons for disobeying Créon's order: 'Je le devais'. This moral imperative is expanded, drawing on the traditional interpretation of the action by Sophocles' heroine ('Ceux qu'on n'enterre pas errent éternellement . . .'), and expressing this in the form of an appeal to the notion of family—even the ill-fated family of Oedipus, whose members are now united in death: a passage whose simple imagery ('Polynice aujourd'hui a achevé sa chasse. Il rentre à la maison . . .') is both eloquent and moving.

There is no doubt that these opening exchanges generate a sympathetic feeling for Antigone, and that Créon's political expediency alienates our sympathy:

> — C'était un révolté et un traître, tu le savais.
> — C'était mon frère.

However, the next 'movement' of the scene[14] is introduced by Créon's acknowledgement that the rough justice of political expediency is not the answer, and that Antigone's motives require a different approach: in his long speech beginning 'L'orgueil d'Oedipe . . .' he changes from a threatening, hectoring approach to a more reflective, more reasonable manner. If his sarcasm at the expense of the 'orgueil d'Oedipe' and of the death-wish of father and daughter, shows his inability to comprehend Antigone's motivation, nevertheless his dignified exposition of his own attitude, his determination to be a 'prince sans histoire', is not lacking in humanity; and his touch of ironic humour in 'si demain un messager crasseux dévale du fond des montagnes . . .' also helps to redress somewhat the balance of sympathy.

The final paragraph of this long speech is still based on the same assumption: that Antigone has made her gesture, and that will be the end of the matter if it can be kept quiet; but Créon is now using a tone of friendly advice ('Tu vas rentrer chez toi . . .') rather than threatening her. The revelation that this second approach is no more effective than the first—represented with graphic economy when Antigone makes to go out of the door which leads back out of the palace, and by the pause that follows—

introduces the next 'movement', which comes nearer to a genuine exchange of views, and to a real attempt on Créon's part to persuade, rather than to browbeat, his adversary.

The attempt at persuasion starts from Antigone's 'il faut faire ce que l'on peut': a confession of obstinate determination in face of absolute power. To argue her out of this attitude, Créon carries out a rational analysis of 'cet enterrement dans les règles': the ceremony is a 'pantomime', performed by mercenary priests, and is lacking in dignity and humanity. At each point Antigone gives way: 'Oui, je les ai vus . . . Si, je l'ai pensé . . . Oui, c'est absurde'—and this last term has at least some of the connotations it possesses in the vocabulary of twentieth-century philosophy. Antigone's defiance is an 'acte gratuit', devoid of rational meaning, and the exchange which follows is one of the most significant of the whole scene:

> — Pourquoi fais-tu ce geste, alors? Pour les autres, pour ceux qui y croient? Pour les dresser contre moi?
> — Non.
> — Ni pour les autres, ni pour ton frère? Pour qui alors?
> — Pour personne. Pour moi.

What had begun as a pious tribute to the dead is now acknowledged as a gratuitous death-wish; and Creon has to admit that although he might have saved Antigone from the penalty of his law, he is powerless to save her from herself. 'J'ai le mauvais rôle, c'est entendu, et tu as le bon': the distribution of sympathy he recognizes is a conventional one, though it is a 'distribution' (to use Le Choeur's term) that has a touch of the melodramatic about it, with its implication of a polarization into black and white. However, we are already aware that the relationship is not as simple as this: Antigone is apparently by no means a reluctant victim, just as Créon is not the conventional villain ('Si j'étais une bonne brute ordinaire de tyran . . .'). And the next 'movement' of the scene is devoted to a thoroughly plausible, and intellectually acceptable, exposition of the 'mauvais rôle' in which he has been cast. This section does not immediately get under way, though: the linking passage in which Créon tries a show of physical strength, while it fits well enough into the context as a demonstration of how a 'brute ordinaire de tyran' might behave, is really justified in theatrical terms as a visual distraction, breaking up this very long dialectical exchange. Similarly, the stage-direction 'Il la fait asseoir . . . Il enlève sa veste . . . en bras de chemise' invests the pause before the next 'movement' of the dialogue with a striking visual character. Créon has stripped off all pretence, as it were, in taking off his jacket, and he will now reveal to Antigone the secrets of his 'métier': a job that is 'ignoble', but which leaves him no choice. The choice that once faced him, as it now faces Antigone, was to say 'yes' or 'no':

> . . . je me suis senti tout d'un coup comme un ouvrier qui refusait un ouvrage. Cela ne m'a pas paru honnête. J'ai dit oui.

The essence of the confrontation between the two characters is the opposition between Créon's 'oui' and Antigone's 'non'—not only a refusal to obey Créon's edict, but a denial of a whole way of life, a rejection of life itself. And it is in this section of the scene that Créon's defence of an ordered, stable society begins to win our intellectual adherence:

> Le cadavre de ton frère qui pourrit sous mes fenêtres, c'est assez payé pour que l'ordre règne dans Thèbes. Mon fils t'aime. Ne m'oblige pas à payer avec toi encore. J'ai assez payé.

And perhaps even more than our intellectual adherence, for his speech beginning 'Mais, bon Dieu! Essaie de comprendre . . .', with its sustained image of the ship of state, forces our admiration for a decent man doing a necessary job of work, however unpalatable. But if Créon has won the spectator over at this point, he has made no impression so far on Antigone herself:

> Je ne veux pas comprendre. C'est bon pour vous. Moi je suis là pour autre chose que pour comprendre. Je suis là pour vous dire non et pour mourir.

We have moved a long way from the confrontation between an authoritarian ruler and a subject prepared to sacrifice her life for a noble cause: the opposition is now between a humane ruler working for his country's good and a rebel motivated by a totally anarchic individualism.

Since Antigone's is not a reasoned stance, but the product of intense emotive feeling, she will be won over, if at all, not by rational but by affective means. And in the next 'movement'—again preceded by a significant pause—what is conceived as a last despairing appeal to her reason ('c'est mon rôle et je vais te faire tuer. Seulement, avant, je veux que toi aussi tu sois bien sûre du tien') almost at once begins to operate on a different level, by reviving intimate recollections of the past, of that childhood which is so important as a nostalgic source of emotional strength to Antigone, and in respect of which she proves so vulnerable. In spite of himself, it seems, Créon's reference to the past hits exactly the right note, as Antigone spontaneously takes over from him with her childhood memories, defending her brother but also providing emotional justification for herself: 'Une fois . . . il était tout pâle, les yeux brillants et si beau dans son vêtement du soir! . . . Et il m'a donné une grande fleur de papier qu'il avait rapportée de sa nuit'. And his intuitive shot in the dark:

> Et tu l'as conservée, n'est-ce pas, cette fleur? Et hier, avant de t'en aller, tu as ouvert ton tiroir et tu l'as regardée, longtemps, pour te donner du courage?

finds the weak spot in her emotional armour:

Antigone tressaille: Qui vous a dit cela?

She is now on the defensive: the 'fleur de cotillon' was the symbol, the 'objective correlative' of her emotional dependence on the past, and this is now to be systematically destroyed. As the graphic catalogue of her brother's moral turpitude and iniquity builds up, her repeated 'Ce n'est pas vrai!' tries to shut out the truth. Almost immediately, however, she is forced to capitulate, and long before the end of Créon's recital she is beaten—not by intellectual persuasion, but by a process of emotional humiliation.

Créon's victory is symbolized visually, after another of the pauses that mark off the stages in this crucial encounter, by Antigone making as if to leave by the other exit: the exit that represents submission, and the acceptance of life on Créon's terms. But it is a short-lived victory; and one of the most convincing touches in the scene is that it should be Créon's better nature—the measure of sympathetic humanity by which Anouilh's character distinguishes himself from his Greek counterpart—that brings about his undoing. His speech 'Rien d'autre ne compte . . .' is certainly motivated by relief that the argument is over: the past tenses ('tu allais le gaspiller . . . je buvais tes paroles. J'écoutais . . .') express this relief, and there is perhaps now also a reflection of the patronizing superiority of the older and wiser man to be seen in the repeated imperatives, the confident future tense of 'Tu verras . . . Tu l'apprendras toi aussi', and the sententious maxims ('Rien n'est vrai que ce qu'on ne dit pas . . . la vie ce n'est peut-être tout de même que le bonheur'). But it would be wrong, I think, to interpret Créon's conciliatory manner here ('j'aurais fait comme toi à vingt ans . . . J'écoutais du fond du temps un petit Créon maigre et pâle comme toi') and his frank confession of expediency ('Ne m'écoute pas quand je ferai mon prochain discours devant le tombeau d'Étéocle. Ce ne sera pas vrai . . .') as a cynical argumentative ploy. For the argument appears to be won; and Créon is inspired not so much by dialectical considerations—not even by the desire to press home his tactical advantage—as by a wholly human urge to make a genuine confession, and to show understanding and fellow-feeling.

And once again, it is not the faulty logic of an argument, but the emotive connotations of a single word, 'le bonheur', that allow Antigone's subjective imagination to take over and reassert her defiant stand. 'Le bonheur' revives Antigone's intransigent opposition to the normal order of things: she is once again recognizable as the blood-sister of those other Anouilh heroes and heroines who similarly reject all thought of compromise and conciliation. 'Quel sera-t-il mon bonheur? . . .': this speech could easily have been spoken by Thérèse in *La Sauvage*; while the notion of an ideal love, inexorable in its demands:

> . . . si Hémon ne doit plus pâlir quand je pâlis, s'il ne doit plus me croire morte quand je suis en retard de cinq minutes, s'il ne doit plus se sentir seul au monde et me détester quand je ris·sans qu'il sache pourquoi . . .

is that to which Orphée subscribes in *Eurydice*. This is the poetic expression of an attitude that forms part of the psychology of all genuine sexual love; but if it is not tempered by other attributes such as tolerance and a sense of proportion, it is inimical to any permanent relationship in the real world. Antigone, however, has now moved out of the range of such common-sense considerations ('Je vous parle de trop loin maintenant, d'un royaume où vous ne pouvez plus entrer . . .'), and Créon's cause is lost for good.

The remainder of the scene is a 'dialogue de sourds'. On the one hand the man of reason, increasingly angry that his advantage has been lost; and on the other, the representative of an irrational anti-life force, exultant in her escape from his domination. It is in the speech already quoted above, which significantly begins with the phrase repeated from *La Sauvage*: 'Vous me dégoûtez tous avec votre bonheur! . . .' that Antigone comes nearest to a rational analysis of the difference that separates her from Créon. His idea of 'le bonheur' is rejected because it depends on a permanent compromise with the pettiness and the squalor of life: Créon and the other conformists and accepters of life are content to put up with 'cette petite chance, pour tous les jours si on n'est pas trop exigeant', whereas Antigone's own notion of 'le bonheur' is the intransigent ideal of an implacable Romantic:

> Moi, je veux tout, tout de suite,—et que ce soit entier,—ou alors je refuse! Je ne veux pas être modeste, moi, et me contenter d'un petit morceau si j'ai été bien sage. Je veux être sûre de tout aujourd'hui et que cela soit aussi beau que quand j'étais petite—ou mourir.

But the last page of the scene shows rational analysis giving way to insult and abuse, Créon threatening and using physical force, and Antigone taunting him with the repeated 'cuisinier', to end on a note of heightened dramatic tension.

(xiii) Antigone, Créon, Ismène (p. 85)

As in Sophocles, the central confrontation is brought to an end by the entrance of Ismène. Anouilh makes less of this scene between the sisters—in the Greek play their argument is expressed in an effective passage of highly dramatic stichomythia—but essentially the purpose is the same: to allow the heroine to assert her independence. Sophocles' 'You chose; life was your choice, when mine was death' (line 481), corresponding to Anouilh's 'Tu as choisi la vie et moi la mort', reminds us once more of the close affinity in the attitude of the two heroines, however different Anouilh's interpretation of that attitude may be. Having rejected her sister's support, Antigone renews her taunting of Créon; and as the women go out, Anouilh brings Le Choeur in for a brief linking scene.

(xiv) Créon, Le Choeur (p. 86)

This considerably reduces the length of the corresponding scene in Sophocles, where a choric ode dwells on the perils lying in wait for those in a position of power: 'For mortals greatly to live is greatly to suffer' (line 531)—a cryptic warning to the wilful and unheeding Creon of the Greek play. Anouilh's Choeur is not so circumspect, with his 'Tu es fou, Créon. Qu'as-tu fait?'; but this direct challenge is met by Créon with a considered defence of his conduct which must carry conviction: 'C'est elle qui voulait mourir . . .'. What he says here—that Polynice's burial was a mere pretext, and that 'Ce qui importait pour elle, c'était de refuser et de mourir'—is surely entirely valid: no other explanation will account for Antigone's behaviour at the end of the scene with Créon, and this is certainly how we are meant to see her exit:

> Antigone, dans un grand cri soulagé: Enfin, Créon!

It seems not unimportant, therefore, that Créon should be provided with the opportunity to justify himself in this way before the scene with Hémon.

(xv) Créon, Hémon, Le Choeur (p. 87)

In the scene with Hémon itself, Créon's self-justification carries less weight, for now his intellectual persuasiveness is countered by the emotional appeal that Hémon makes to the spectator: a good deal less ambivalent than that made by the heroine, for his reaction to the threatened loss of his beloved has none of the arbitrary quality of her voluntary rejection of life. This is another scene that closely follows the inspiration of its Greek counterpart—though here too the French playwright has seen fit to reduce the length of the original, where both father and son speak in terms of measured debate before engaging in angry stichomythia. It is not clear why Anouilh should make Le Choeur intervene here as he does ('Est-ce qu'on ne peut pas imaginer quelque chose . . . Est-ce qu'on ne peut pas gagner du temps?'), except perhaps that the Greek Chorus also intervenes, though in a much less partisan spirit. In the French play as in the Greek, the scene mounts to a dramatic climax—a more affective climax in Anouilh's case, for Hémon, as Antigone has done, draws emotional reinforcement from the evocation of the past: 'Tu es encore puissant, toi, comme lorsque j'étais petit. Ah! je t'en supplie, père, que je t'admire, que je t'admire encore! Je suis trop seul et le monde est trop nu si je ne peux pas t'admirer'. The young man's emotional anguish is helpless against the resigned pragmatism of his father, however: 'Regarde-moi, c'est cela devenir un homme, voir le visage de son père en face un jour'. But where the Greek Haemon rushes out at the height of an angry explosion, and with Creon's vindictive threat ringing in his ears, Anouilh's character goes out in frustrated bewilderment to fulfil his tragic role.

(xvi) Créon, Le Choeur (p. 89)

And the only difference between the attitude of Créon and that of Le Choeur is that the latter, no omniscient commentator now, but a participant whose function is much nearer to that of the Greek Chorus, still hopes that some way may be found of averting the tragedy ('Créon, il faut faire quelque chose'). It is Créon, not le Choeur, who now seems to possess a compassionate insight into the tragic process.

(xvii) Créon, Antigone, Les Gardes, Le Choeur (p. 89)

As she does in Sophocles, Antigone makes a final reappearance before she goes to her death. But whereas the corresponding scene in the Greek play presents a moving exchange between the heroine and the Chorus:

> — But here is a sight beyond all bearing,
> At which my eyes cannot but weep;
> Antigone forth faring
> To her bridal-bower of endless sleep.
> — You see me, countrymen, on my last journey,
> Taking my last leave of the light of day;
> Going to my rest, where death shall take me
> Alive across the silent river . . . (lines 708–15)

Anouilh's purpose is to underline the pathos by other means; and after a brief linking scene, Antigone is left alone with Le Garde.

(xviii) Antigone, Le Garde (p. 90)

As in the scenes with La Nourrice, the playwright has deliberately chosen at this point to adopt a tone at variance with what one traditionally expects of serious tragic drama; but here, the challenge of the familiar, colloquial style is a much more difficult one. For in the earlier scenes the nostalgic evocation of the heroine's childhood not only generates the sympathy that we feel for her in the initial stages of her clash with Créon, it also defines the vital emotional resources on which she will draw in that encounter. In this closing scene, we may assume that the author's purpose is to reinforce the poignancy of Antigone's approaching death by juxtaposing it with the ordinary banalities of life; but if the lowering of the emotional tone, and the adoption of such a colloquial stylistic register, fails to strike the right note, it can easily lead to the dissipation of the spectator's sympathy. This is in an acute form the problem that faces every author of tragic drama in a domestic idiom.

The scene opens with the emotionally charged 'Mon dernier visage d'homme'; we may compare 'la dernière folie . . .' (p. 56), and two instances of 'pour la dernière fois' (pp. 78, 88), that fateful phrase which has such a powerful tragic resonance whenever it occurs as a half-line in Racine's verse: even in Anouilh's prose, it is impossible to mistake the emotional potential of the repeated 'dernier'. But at once the level of the dialogue drops to that of everyday conversation. It is not a case of intrinsically comic, or caricatural, characterization: the portrait of this very ordinary soldier, with his military slang, his self-importance, and his obsession with pay and perquisites, is thoroughly lifelike, and any comic effect derives from the incongruity between his very ordinariness and the high drama of the preceding scenes. The longer the exchanges go on, the greater will be the risk that the verbose, repetitive parade of trivia will neutralize the dramatic tension that has built up to its climax—or that the spectator will take refuge in laughter as a relief from that tension.

From Antigone's 'Je vais mourir tout à l'heure', the focus is no longer on Le Garde. For a moment she is unable to break through his self-absorption, but her question 'Comment vont-ils me faire mourir?' succeeds in reestablishing genuine communication. However, contact is abruptly broken again with her exclamation 'O tombeau! O lit nuptial! O ma demeure souterraine!'—a version of Sophocles'

> So to my grave,
> My bridal-bower, my everlasting prison,
> I go, to join those many of my kinsmen
> Who dwell in the mansions of Persephone. (lines 769–72)

The change to such a strikingly different mode of expression symbolizes her retreat into her own private sensibility. The beginning of Le Garde's next speech, with its mythological allusion ('Aux cavernes de Hadès . . .') is not too incongruous, but in no time at all he lapses into more of his trite observations on the military life.

The second half of this scene, which is taken up with Antigone's attempt to dictate a farewell letter to Hémon, is a masterly invention on Anouilh's part. The heroine's loss of the certainty and self-confidence she had shown when facing Créon ('je ne sais plus pourquoi je meurs . . .'), the revelation of how near she came to being won over by him, can only be expressed in a confessional medium equivalent to the classical soliloquy; and in addition to the imaginative realization of such an equivalent, Anouilh has created a scene which offers the theatrically effective counterpoint between Antigone's intimate self-analysis ('Il vaut mieux que jamais personne ne sache. C'est comme s'ils devaient me voir nue et me toucher quand je serai morte') and the clumsy insensitivity of Le Garde ('C'est une drôle de lettre'). This is another scene which to the reader may perhaps seem to border on the facile and the over-sentimental; one can only say that it is capable of working successfully in the theatre, as a vehicle for genuinely-felt emotion.

(xix) Le Messager, Le Choeur (p. 95)

The elimination of the scene with Tiresias, which occurs at this point in the Greek play, is quite the most significant change introduced by Anouilh. Not only does it go a long way towards abolishing the role of the gods, and depriving the myth of its metaphysical dimension; it also has an important effect on the characterization of Créon. For the result of this scene is that Sophocles' King belatedly takes steps to undo what he has done, though of course he is too late to save Antigone. Anouilh's Créon undergoes no such change of heart: there is no mouthpiece of the gods to persuade him, and he remains unrepentant to the end.

From this point on in Anouilh's play, the final events happen even more rapidly than in Sophocles. Le Messager is less prolix and sententious than his Greek counterpart, though the vital detail of his narrative is taken over unchanged:

> His son looked at him with one angry stare,
> Spat in his face, and then without a word
> Drew sword and struck out. But his father fled
> Unscathed. Whereon the poor demented boy
> Leaned on his sword and thrust it deeply home
> In his own side, and while his life ebbed out
> Embraced the maid in loose-enfolding arms,
> His spurting blood staining her pale cheeks red. (lines 1076–83)

> . . . Il regarde son père sans rien dire, une minute, et, tout à coup, il lui crache au visage, et tire son épée. Créon a bondi hors de portée. Alors Hémon le regarde avec ses yeux d'enfant, lourds de mépris, et Créon ne peut pas éviter ce regard comme la lame. Hémon regarde ce vieil homme tremblant à l'autre bout de la caverne et, sans rien dire, il se plonge l'épée dans le ventre et il s'étend contre Antigone, l'embrassant dans une immense flaque rouge.

(xx) Créon, Le Page, Le Choeur (p. 96)

In what is presumably a deliberate change designed to produce a greater measure of sympathy for Créon at the end of the play, the closing lines spoken by Sophocles' Messenger, with their implication of Creon's guilt:

> Two bodies lie together, wedded in death,
> Their bridal sleep a witness to the world
> How great a calamity can come to man
> Through man's perversity (lines 1084–7)

are transferred to Créon himself:

> Je les ai fait coucher l'un près de l'autre, enfin! Ils sont lavés, maintenant, reposés. Ils sont seulement un peu pâles, mais si calmes. Deux amants. Ils ont fini, eux

—a passage in which it may not be too fanciful to see, as well as the transposition of Sophocles' text, an echo of the end of *Romeo and Juliet*.

Finally, le Choeur takes over for the narration of the death of Eurydice: one of the passages that stand out by their anachronistic detail, and a passage that can surely be criticized for its unwarranted trivialization of the original. A bourgeois Queen who does good works for the poor of Thebes, and who methodically finishes off her row of knitting before going away to commit suicide: is this successful modernization of the context, or a glaring lapse of taste? The same points apply as have been made in the commentary on scene xviii; this is, after all, the emotional climax of the play, and that it is not merely a question of old-fashioned, narrow standards of taste is suggested by Bergson's perceptive remark about laughter: 'Est comique tout incident qui appelle notre attention sur le physique d'une personne alors que le moral est en cause'[15].

(xxi) Le Choeur (p. 97)

The last section of this scene, together with the final scene in which Le Choeur appears on his own, are devoted to closing the 'frame' in which the death of Antigone has been presented, by re-establishing the continuum of ordinary life that had been disrupted by the violent events. 'La journée a été rude': the spectator, like the characters who have participated in the 'rude journée', has earned the right to rest. But for Créon, the active protagonist, there can be no rest ('devant l'ouvrage, on ne peut pourtant pas se croiser les bras . . .'); and he goes off to his council meeting. He has opted for life, he has a responsibility for others, and he must see it through to the end. This is more than just passive resignation to the continuity of things; and Créon's active acceptance of such a commitment can be seen as representing that reaffirmation of positive values after the destructive force of the tragic event has spent itself, that seems to be a necessary condition for the 'purging of the passions' traditionally associated with tragedy, and that can be clearly illustrated in such diverse examples as *Hamlet*, *King Lear*, *Phèdre* or *La Machine infernale*. We do not feel emotional involvement with Créon at this point, any more than we do with Albany, Fortinbras, Racine's Thésée or Cocteau's Tirésias, who similarly 'close the frame', rounding-off the tragic process. We respect and (possibly) admire him, but our position is closer to that invoked by Le Choeur: the position of those for whom normal existence can resume (as it will for us as we leave the theatre), but whose life has, in spite of themselves, been marked by the impact of 'la petite Antigone':

> Sans la petite Antigone, c'est vrai, ils auraient tous été bien tranquilles. Mais maintenant, c'est fini. Ils sont tout de même tranquilles. . . .

For those who understood nothing, there is nothing to forget. Nothing has changed, and life will carry on as before: the Gardes 'continuent à jouer aux cartes'. Yet although this is the image that we are left with as the curtain falls, it does not determine our attitude as spectators, and we cannot identify with characters so incapable of reflection. Our affinity is with 'ceux qui vivent encore', who have come through the tragic anguish to a new serenity. With the passage of time we too may, as Le Choeur suggests, gradually begin 'à les oublier et à confondre leurs noms'; but for the time being 'Un grand apaisement triste tombe sur Thèbes'—and this is by no means an unsuccessful attempt to define the position of the spectator, whose 'tristesse' is also 'apaisée', but not yet eliminated, by the return to normality that forms an essential part of the cathartic process.

VI Antigone *in 1944*

The study of the reception of Anouilh's play in 1944, and of its relationship to the political situation which existed, first under the German occupation and then after the liberation of Paris, has become much easier since the publication of an important monograph on the subject by Manfred Flügge[16]. Quite apart from the unusually broad range of Dr Flügge's enquiry, which sets *Antigone* in the general context of political attitudes current in France in the 1930s and 40s, he has accumulated an invaluable compendium of critical comment on the play from reviews and other ephemeral sources; moreover, he has had the rare good fortune (not vouchsafed to all who have written on

Anouilh and his work, by any means) to elicit from the playwright himself a
valuable commentary on the origins of the play.

From Anouilh's own indications—corrected by Flügge's research, where
the dramatist's memory proved fallible—it now seems likely that the
stimulus for the composition of *Antigone* (which, it was already known,
existed in a complete state as early as 1942) came from the case of a young
resistance fighter, Paul Collette, who in August 1942 fired on a group of
collaborationist leaders at an anti-communist legionaries' rally at Versailles,
severely wounding Marcel Déat and Pierre Laval. The connection appears all
the more convincing if one considers the comment of a resistance journal:

> Paul Collette s'estimait mandaté par sa conscience de Français. Il
> n'appartenait à aucun réseau. A aucun mouvement politique . . . Personne ni
> aucun mouvement ne pouvait, au regard de l'Histoire, expliquer le mobile de
> sa mission. Il s'agissait de l'acte gratuit dans toute la noblesse du terme. Ce
> jeune homme allait improviser un attentat. (I, p. 234)

Completed in 1942, the play received the approval of the German censor; and
the delay of two years before its first performance appears to have been due to
André Barsacq, whose production of *Eurydice* had been only moderately
successful, and who was unwilling to risk further financial liabilities. When
production did go ahead, there was no need to seek further permission for a
text which already bore the official stamp of approval; and the only diffi-
culties raised during the first run of the play came from a report received in
Berlin to the effect that *Antigone* was not suitable entertainment for the
occupation troops. Barsacq was able to resist attempts to suspend performances, and the play ran without interruption from February until August.

'N'y allez pas, c'est une pièce nazie' was, it appears, a common reaction in
resistance circles; and among those ordinary playgoers who did see *Antigone*
in 1944 there must have been a large proportion who thought like this
writer:

> L'auteur, ai-je pensé, n'est pas sans amour ni pitié pour son Antigone, mais il
> est franchement du côté de Créon, et c'est à lui qu'il donne raison. J'ai même
> pensé, sommairement: 'Créon, c'est Laval'.

And even where the interpretation was less positive, there is abundant
evidence that a great deal of the play's appeal lay in its highly provocative
topicality:

> Pour nous, le débat était dans l'opposition entre mystique et politique,
> surtout dans ce que cette opposition avait de brûlant à l'époque: en clair,
> Créon, pour nous, c'était Pétain, à qui se heurtait l'intransigeance de ceux qui
> n'admettaient pas le compromis et que représentait Antigone. Mais il nous

semblait qu'Anouilh ne donnait pas entièrement tort à Créon. Il n'y a peut-
être pas de pièce dont nous ayons autant discuté'. (I, p. 268)

Looking back on this era, G. Hanoteau writes of a 'dialogue de sourds':

> Les uns n'avaient entendu que Créon et l'antique légende se mettant au
> service . . . de la Collaboration, alors que leurs adversaires n'avaient retenu
> que les révoltes d'Antigone, première 'résistante' avec vingt-cinq siècles
> d'avance. (I, p. 267)

When we come to the interpretations of *Antigone* published in the press of
the period, we can see how Anouilh's play was regularly annexed by both
pro-German and resistance writers 'pour les besoins de la cause'. In such a
highly-charged political atmosphère as that of occupied Paris, the favourable
notices from reviewers of a known collaborationist tendency could be far
more harmful than any adverse criticism. Indeed, a source of some of the
most damaging accusations after the liberation of Paris was the extremely
favourable reviews *Antigone* had received from Alain Laubreaux, a notable
collaborator, who wrote no fewer than four laudatory pieces. While
admiring the characterization of the heroine, this reviewer had seen in her 'la
révolte de la pureté contre les mensonges des hommes, de l'âme contre la vie,
une révolte insensée et magnifique, mais terriblement dangereuse pour
l'espèce puisque dans la vie des sociétés elle aboutit au désordre et au chaos, et
dans la vie des êtres elle aboutit au suicide' (*Je suis partout*); and in similar
terms in another journal he wrote: 'Révolte condamnable puisqu'elle aboutit
au chaos dans l'ordre social et au suicide dans l'ordre organique' (*Le Petit
Parisien*) (II, pp. 49–50). Laubreaux' praise is repeated, and indeed amplified,
by Charles Méré in *Aujourd'hui*, another journal with collaborationist
sympathies:

> . . . Dans la pièce de M. Jean Anouilh, le héros, c'est au contraire Créon, le
> roi juste, esclave de son devoir et qui doit aux intérêts de sa patrie sacrifier
> ses affections les plus chères. . . . En face de Créon, victime pitoyable
> de la tragédie, l'inintelligence d'Antigone fait figure de demi-folle, de
> dégénérée. . . . C'est la révoltée, l'anarchiste, génératrice de désordre, de
> désastre, de mort. (II, p. 57)

It was not only interpretations of the play in a specific political sense that
could be damaging, but the very fact of a favourable review in certain
publications: for instance, the notice by J. de Féraudy in *Au Pilori*, a notori-
ously anti-semitic journal. And as disturbing as anything at this period must
have been Anouilh's inclusion, in an article by L. Rebatet in *Je suis partout*, in
a list of writers who, 's'ils ne font pas de politique, ne répugnent point
pourtant à publier leurs oeuvres dans les journaux où on en fait beaucoup, et
de plus énergiquement anti-gaulliste' (I, p. 308).

Until the liberation of Paris, the attack from the spokesmen of the resistance was confined to the organs of the clandestine press; and it was an article
by Claude Roy of March 1944 that contained the most virulent denunciation
of Anouilh as a playwright who had betrayed the resistance fighters by his
travesty of the 'true' Antigone:

> Sur les murs de Paris, le seul nom d'Antigone semble un appel, un camouflet à
> l'oppresseur de Vichy, au nazi qui passe devant l'affiche rouge et jaune de
> l'Atelier. Antigone ou la fidélité. Antigone proclame à la face du tyran qu'on
> peut mourir pour la justice, mourir pour la fidélité, mourir pour les valeurs
> qui donnent à la vie un prix, au destin un sens.
>
>   Antigone, lisons-nous. Au-delà d'Antigone, notre pensée déjà va vers tous
> ceux qui, chaque jour, meurent pour que vive leur honneur, leur vérité et leur
> patrie. Mais il s'agit de bien d'autre chose. Non de Sophocle, mais de Jean
> Anouilh. Et l'Antigone qu'on nous propose n'est pas *notre* Antigone, la seule,
> la vraie. Antigone-de-la-pureté.

For Anouilh's heroine, like Créon, 'méprise les hommes':

> Parce qu'il les méprise, Créon les opprime et les mate. Le tyran glacé et la
> jeune exaltée étaient faits pour s'entendre. Si Antigone pouvait vivre, à force
> de dire 'Non' à la vie, elle dirait 'Oui' à tout. Sa mort n'est pas l'affirmation
> d'un héroïsme, mais un refus et un suicide. C'est moins un acte qu'un
> malentendu.

And the reason for such a portrayal is that Anouilh is one of those '. . .
anciens loups qui ont accepté avec empressement le collier du chien, du chien
policier':

> Ce n'est pas un hasard qui les fait parfois, prudemment, s'enrôler sous le
> drapeau noir de la Waffen SS . . . Ce n'est pas un hasard qui fait de Jean
> Anouilh des *Pièces noires* un collaborateur occasionnel mais fervent de la feuille
> nazie, un admirateur naïf et femmelin du Führer et de son génie. (II,
> pp. 70–1)

It is certain that Anouilh had to live through a most uncomfortable time
during the period of 'l'épuration': the hasty and badly managed 'purge' of
writers and other public figures whose record under the Occupation had not
been untarnished, which under the guise of political justice allowed the
settling of many an old score of a personal nature. Though his name never
appeared on any known 'black list', there were certainly moves to discredit
him at the time of the *reprise* of *Antigone* at the end of September 1944, and a
letter was sent to Barsacq by the 'Commission pour l'épuration des théâtres',
with the object of forcing him to withdraw from the direction of this revival.
However, the play was in fact staged again, and Anouilh confesses in his
letter to Flügge that it was at this point, not at the time of the first

performances under the Occupation, that 'les vrais ennuis pour nous . . . ont commencé'. He describes the first performance of the revival as follows:

> . . . Personne n'a osé applaudir à la fin jusqu'à ce que le Général Koenig [a Free French associate of de Gaulle, now military governor of Paris] se lève dans sa loge et crie: 'C'est admirable!' C'est ce qui m'a sauvé. Le reste n'a été qu'insinuations méchantes. (II, p. 45)

From all this, it must be abundantly clear that it was extremely difficult, if not impossible, to approach *Antigone* in 1944 completely without political prejudice, and to judge it purely and simply as a work of art. Pol Gaillard's verdict, published in the Communist *L'Humanité* in November of that year, is a good example of an aesthetic judgement determined by political and moral considerations:

> Disons-le nettement puisqu'il reste encore des doutes, paraît-il: l'*Antigone* de Jean Anouilh n'est pas un chef-d'oeuvre, et elle ne peut que faire du mal aux Français. . . . Rien ne pouvait mieux servir les desseins nazis pendant l'occupation; rien ne peut davantage freiner le relèvement des Français par eux-mêmes aujourd'hui encore. . . . Malgré ses beautés, *Antigone* restera, dans l'oeuvre de M. Anouilh, non seulement un faux chef-d'oeuvre, mais une mauvaise action. (I, p. 320)

And evidence of the effect of such tendentious criticism, as well as of the more balanced view that it was possible to adopt a mere three years later, is to be seen in this comment by Robert Kemp in 1947:

> Quand fut représentée, en février 1944, l'*Antigone* de M. Jean Anouilh . . ., je n'ai eu ni l'occasion ni un désir vif de l'entendre. Des bruits, que je peux maintenant dire absurdes, me la faisaient croire trop conciliante pour mon goût. Or, c'est une oeuvre pure et dure, qui accepte sans doute avec plus d'indulgence que la tragédie de Sophocle le pragmatisme de Créon, mais sans qu'on y puisse découvrir le moindre esprit de complicité à l'égard de ce qui se passait alors dans notre personnel provisoirement dirigeant. (I, p. 326)

What, finally, of Anouilh's own position at this period? It really does seem to be the case that, as Béatrice Dussane was to write, 'Anouilh est resté pendant toute l'Occupation confiné dans son travail d'écrivain, professant qu'il ignorait volontairement la politique' (I, p. 369). Difficult though this may be to accept as entirely valid, it certainly matches his own explanation in the letter to Flügge, where he says of his attitude at the time of the first performances of *Antigone*: 'à la création, dans ma naïveté un peu ahurie d'homme qui s'est toujours senti libre—je n'avais pas eu le sentiment de risquer quelque chose' (II, p. 45).

But a mere twelve months after the première of *Antigone*, Anouilh's naïve idealism came to an abrupt end. One of the victims of the 'épuration' was

Robert Brasillach, a poet, critic and journalist, who had made himself enemies by his collaborationist activities during the Occupation, and who was tried and condemned to death. For Anouilh, who hardly knew Brasillach, this seems to have been a major turning-point in his life. He was moved to take a petition round to fellow men of letters, seeking signatures for the commutation of the death penalty: an act by no means lacking in courage, if one thinks of the playwright's own ambiguous situation at this very time. The petition was unsuccessful, and Brasillach was executed in February 1945:

> En y réfléchissant depuis, rassis, sceptique, navré (au sens fort du terme) et étrangement allégé par l'âge, je me suis aperçu que le jeune homme que j'ai été et le jeune homme Brasillach sont morts le même jour et—toutes proportions gardées—de la même chose.
>
> Tout cela est loin—et tout près. Le jeune homme Anouilh que j'étais resté, jusqu'en 1945, est parti un matin, mal assuré (il y avait de quoi en ces temps d'imposture), mais du pied gauche, pour aller recueillir les signatures de ses confrères pour Brasillach. Il a fait du porte à porte pendant huit jours et il est revenu vieux chez lui. . .[17].

VII   *Anouilh's Theatre since* Antigone

From a strict point of view, any consideration of Anouilh's theatre since *Antigone* might seem to be irrelevant to the study of that play. On the other hand, the recurrence of similar themes and attitudes may not be totally without importance in helping to determine our interpretation of *Antigone* itself; while more generally, it is interesting to see how these same themes and attitudes have been modified as the playwright moved on through the post-war period and through his own middle age.

First, a fragment of an unfinished *Oreste*, published in 1945—though apparently written in 1942, the same year as *Antigone*[18]—provides further evidence of the fascination that the Greek myths exercised on Anouilh at a certain stage in his career: in particular the Orestes myth, which was also attracting Sartre at very much the same time. The most interesting aspect of the fragment is that it reveals such a similar approach to the question of modernizing a subject from antiquity: the same deliberate anachronisms, the same juxtaposition of serious and trivial, as we have seen in *Antigone*:

> *Électre*: Quelquefois la nuit, je descendais dans la cuisine, je prenais tous les bassins, tous les plats de fer et je les lâchais tous à la fois sur la pierre . . .

Oreste sourit malgré lui: Petite peste!

Électre lui crie: Tu les entendais, Égisthe? Tu les entendais de ta chambre?

Égisthe doucement: Oui. Mais ils ne faisaient pas autant de bruit que mon souvenir.

Moreover, the playwright has approached the problem of dealing with a known subject in very much the same way as in *Antigone*, creating an effect similar to that produced by the Prologue in the opening speech of that play:

Égisthe s'avance: Voilà. Nous sommes là tous les quatre sous le soleil, dans cette ombre étroite et puante au pied des murs d'Argos et nous allons jouer le jeu d'Électre et d'Oreste—le jeu d'Égisthe et de Clytemnestre. Un jeu terrible où tous les coups sont bons. Quatre joueurs et une balle rouge qu'on se relance inlassablement et qui brûle les mains et du sang par terre où l'on patauge; un terrain détrempé de sang. Deux hommes et deux femmes ou plutôt un homme et une femme—et deux enfants. Et le résultat de la partie écrit de toute éternité sur un immense panneau derrière les joueurs en lettres grandes comme les hommes. C'est comme cela qu'on joue bien. Moi, je suis Égisthe, l'amant de Clytemnestre.

Clytemnestre: Moi, je suis Clytemnestre.

Oreste: Moi, je suis Oreste.

Électre crie: Moi, je suis Électre!

Égisthe: Elle l'a crié. Elle criera pendant toute la partie. Elle est trop jeune. Elle ne sait pas encore très bien le jeu. . . .

However, there is something so schematic, so almost mechanical, in the way the formula is used here that the effect is one of self-parody; and it is difficult to believe that if the play had been completed along these lines, *Oreste* could ever have been defended against the charge of gratuitous trivialization.

Médée is a different matter. Published in 1946 in the *Nouvelles Pièces noires* (together with *Jézabel*, *Antigone* and *Roméo et Jeannette*) and performed in 1953, this play represents the last of this group of experiments with a Greek subject[19]. It is a much slighter play than *Eurydice* or *Antigone*, and less interesting, no doubt, from a technical point of view. Anouilh has been more discreet in his anachronisms, but there is an uneasy tension between the prosaic colloquialism of some of the dialogue and the daemonic character of the legendary sorceress and murderer, which is well brought out in the magnificent incantatory invocation to Evil, a soliloquy of great poetic force:

C'est maintenant, Médée, qu'il faut être toi-même . . . O mal! Grande bête vivante qui rampe sur moi et me lèche, prends-moi. Je suis à toi cette nuit, je suis ta femme. Pénètre-moi, déchire-moi, gonfle et brûle au milieu de moi. Tu vois, je t'accueille, je t'aide, je m'ouvre . . . Pèse sur moi de ton grand corps velu, serre-moi dans tes grandes mains calleuses, ton souffle rauque sur ma bouche, étouffe-moi. Je vis enfin! Je souffre et je nais. Ce sont mes noces. C'est pour cette nuit d'amour avec toi que j'ai vécu.

There are recognizable echoes of earlier plays in a passage like the following, in spite of the aggressive crudity of the imagery:

> Nourrice, nourrice, je suis grosse ce soir. J'ai mal et j'ai peur comme lorsque tu m'aidais à me tirer un petit de mon ventre . . . Aide-moi, nourrice! Quelque chose bouge dans moi comme autrefois et c'est quelque chose qui dit non à leur joie à eux là-bas, c'est quelque chose qui dit non au bonheur.

But there is an interesting shift of sympathy, which provides an important pointer to future developments. Médée herself, who has obvious affinities with Anouilh's élite caste of intransigent idealists, has sacrificed everything for Jason in the past, and now insists that he continue to sacrifice everything for her. Logically, her claim is undeniable, just as Jason's desertion of her is indefensible. But Médée's arrogant rejection of all the values of the world around her alienates much of the sympathy we might be prepared to feel even for this arch-criminal, and we are more inclined to side with Jason the opportunist, when he says:

> Poursuis ta course. Tourne en rond, déchire-toi, bats-toi, méprise, insulte, tue, refuse tout ce qui n'est pas toi. Moi, je m'arrête. Je me contente. J'accepte ces apparences aussi durement, aussi résolument que je les ai refusées autrefois avec toi. Et s'il faut continuer à se battre, c'est pour elles maintenant que je me battrai, humblement, adossé à ce mur dérisoire, construit de mes mains entre le néant absurde et moi.

In *Antigone*, if Créon's argument wins our intellectual support, our emotional sympathy remains with Antigone; here, the formula is almost reversed, and Jason claims at least a major share of our sympathy.

In the plays from 1950 onwards, there are two further instances in which an uncompromising idealist of the type familiar to us from the earlier period is given the 'beau rôle'. These are Anouilh's plays on the historical subjects of Joan of Arc and Thomas Becket; and in the motivation of the heroine of *L'Alouette* (1952) and the hero of *Becket* (1958)—partly dedication to a cause greater than themselves, partly subjective self-fulfilment—can be seen, *mutatis mutandis*, a clear echo of the motives of Antigone. But in contrast to this direct evolution, there is a concurrent series of plays—*Colombe* (1950), *Ornifle* (1955), *Pauvre Bitos* (1956)—in which attitudes which have a recognizable affinity with those of earlier heroes are devalued and shown in an unsympathetic or ridiculous light. More important still, from this same period onwards, in a series of plays looking forward to Anouilh's more recent production, the balance of sympathy was being tipped towards a new kind of central figure—the word 'hero' is perhaps no longer appropriate —who chooses the course of acceptance rather than of renunciation.

The retired generals of *Ardèle* (1948), *La Valse des Toréadors* (1951) and

L'Hurluberlu (1956) all retain something of their youthful idealism—they have not quite given up their quest for a cause—but experience has taught them that it is wiser to adapt to life, with its imperfections and its constant disappointments. As Le Général says in *Ardèle*: 'Il y a l'amour, bien sûr. Et puis il y a la vie, son ennemie'. Instead of opting for the exigencies of an ideal love, the new-style Anouilh hero is a pragmatist who makes do with the realities of life. Love is bound to be destroyed by contact with reality; family relationships are a source of frustration, deceit and pain; but the unheroic heroes of a whole series of plays from *Ne réveillez pas Madame* (1964) through to *Chers Zoiseaux* (1976), *La Culotte* (1978) and *Le Nombril* (1981), have all chosen to make the best of a bad job. And in spite of a certain moral ambiguity which sometimes almost suggests those arch-compromisers, the fathers in *La Sauvage* and *Eurydice*, they also have something of Jason and even of Créon in their ancestry.

At first sight there may not seem to be much in common between Créon and the central characters of these recent plays, usually disillusioned novelists or men of the theatre with a distinct autobiographical, or confessional, element in their make-up, who are trying to reconcile the demands of their professional and their private lives. But Créon's closing line: 'Eh bien, si nous avons conseil, petit, nous allons y aller', like Jason's 'je me battrai, humblement, adossé à ce mur dérisoire, construit de mes mains entre le néant absurde et moi', indicates an important link. Heroism—the modified heroism of the older Anouilh—is now seen to lie in the stoical acceptance, not the futile rejection, of life. Human dignity—self-respect, if not always the respect of others—depends on the conscientious performance of the job one is called on to do; and what these later characters—and, we may add, their creator himself—share with Créon is the determination to maintain a kind of human dignity in the face of the injustice, the pain and the absurdity of existence.

VIII   Antigone *Today*

As well as arousing intense political passions on its first appearance in 1944, *Antigone* also provoked extreme judgements on artistic grounds. The principal sticking-point was the question of Anouilh's deliberate anachronisms, which appeared to some contemporary commentators to be cheap, meretricious, and incompatible with a serious re-working of the Greek subject. Even those reviews which praised the play on other grounds frequently expressed reservations on this score; and the following comments represent the dominant tone of contemporary opinion as analysed by Flügge: '[Anouilh] encanaille tout à loisir'; 'l'anachronisme est devenu la Muse numéro un du théâtre d'avant-garde . . . Est-ce qu'on ne pourrait pas, maintenant, la laisser reposer un petit peu?'; 'il y a là un parti pris qui nous déplaît'; '. . . facilités inutiles'; 'l'excentricité facile de certains anachronismes'; 'avec quelques anachronismes faciles, ce diable de Jean Anouilh frôle parfois le mauvais goût'; 'de puérils artifices . . . banalités dans le style bernsteinien . . . faute de goût' (Flügge, II, pp. 51–63). If the thoroughly adverse opinion of the critic of *Comoedia* in 1944:

> Jamais nous n'avons assisté à un spectacle aussi pénible, aussi cruellement ridicule et vide de sens (II, p. 51)

was far from representative, at the same time there were several reviewers who qualified a more favourable judgement by suggesting that Anouilh had failed in his attempt to capture the spirit of genuine tragedy; and the features of the play on which such a judgement depends seem above all to have been the tone: that is to say not only the anachronisms, but also the other ways in which the text of Sophocles' *Antigone* has systematically been brought down to an everyday level; the apportioning of sympathy between the two main protagonists; and the motivation of the heroine's action.

As regards the tone of the play, audiences and reading public of the 1980s are much less ready to take offence at—or even to see anything remarkable in—either the anachronisms or the more general 'lowering' of the literary level in *Antigone* than were the first spectators. There has been a wholesale evolution of taste during the last forty years, brought about in the theatre by playwrights such as Ionesco, Genet and Arrabal, and helped by practitioners in the cinema and in television. Indeed, to a generation educated on a diet of post-war culture the very concept of 'good taste' must seem old-fashioned, if not out-dated; and the notion that tragedy depends on a homogeneous elevation of literary tone is quite incompatible with creative writing in a modern idiom of which incongruity seems to be one of the constants. Anouilh himself has made his own modest contribution to this evolution of taste, and features of *Antigone* which did perhaps shock in 1944 have almost become part of a new orthodoxy. On the other hand, if today's spectators accept—even if they look for—suggestive anachronisms in any re-working of a classical theme, the point made by Robert Brasillach remains valid:

> Ce n'est pas le fait de l'anachronisme qui me gêne parfois dans cette pièce, c'est sa qualité: un peu trop de tendresse, de sentimentalisme, voire de mièvrerie. (II, p. 65)

If unity of tone, in the sense of the literary homogeneity of a text, is now devalued as a criterion of aesthetic judgement, the same is surely not true of unity of emotional tone. Both what Brasillach calls 'le sentimentalisme', and a misplaced emphasis on the concrete details of material existence, run the risk of trivializing the subject, and of dissipating the emotional intensity that it is capable of generating, and at which Anouilh, no less than Sophocles, was surely aiming. This is not a question of literary, or theatrical, fashion, but of the involvement, or empathy, that serious drama—not to beg the question by using the term 'tragedy'—requires us to feel with one or more of the characters on stage. It needs the skilful touch of a master-craftsman (and the equally sure touch of sensitive performers) for serious dialogue to assimilate the trivial and the familiar without becoming either bathetic or comic; and we may all wonder whether Antigone's concern for the fate of her dog after her death, or Queen Eurydice finishing her row of knitting before departing to commit suicide, do not put an undesirable strain on the audience's emotional involvement.

With these minor reservations, Anouilh's transposition of Sophocles into a modern idiom must be accounted one of the most successful of the twentieth-century versions of Greek originals. It is the one example to find favour with George Steiner, a stern critic in whose view 'variations on classic themes have yielded eccentric and often ignoble results. Where the dead gods have been summoned back to the modern footlights, they have brought with them the odour of decay'. The one exception, *Antigone*, does, says Steiner, 'adjust the ancient with the modern, illuminating both'. He sees this as a special case, because of the status of the play as political allegory: 'Political fact gave to the legend a grim relevance. . . . Thus the antique mask served as a true visage of the times' (pp. 330–1). Even at the time Steiner was writing, however, this was to take for granted a context that could be recreated only by a conscious effort of the imagination on the part of a new generation of French readers and playgoers, to say nothing of their counterparts outside France. While such an imaginative reconstruction may provide a valuable extra dimension for the audiences of the 1980s, it can no longer be the main basis of our interpretation.

Audiences who have grown up in post-war France—or outside France —certainly do not find it impossible to identify emotionally with the heroine. Among the young intellectuals she still has kindred spirits, even if for different reasons from those which motivated their parents' sympathy; and the young neo-Romantics of the late 1960s and 70s, for whom instinctive feelings were more potent than intellectual persuasion, were more likely to be attracted than alienated by the nihilistic nature of her arbitrary gesture.

'Il est vrai qu'Antigone m'agace': so commented the playwright himself, looking back in 1967 on his heroine of twenty-five years earlier (McIntyre

p. 130), And no doubt many of us, whose emotional sympathies were roused by Antigone when we were more or less of an age with the heroine herself, now find Créon more persuasive than we did. But most of us will never be won over completely by Créon's logic—any more than we were ever able completely to identify with Antigone in her instinctive self-immolation. That Anouilh himself had not gone over to Créon's side is shown in the last paragraph of one of the pieces he was to write, looking back on the Brasillach affair—a moving testimony to the values that had inspired the writing of *Antigone* in 1942:

> Ce n'est pas la mort qui tue et souille, malgré le sang qui coule et la boue d'hiver où l'on tombe. Quand la salve inutile éclate, l'homme qui a signé la sentence s'écroule, commençant sa putréfaction et promenant son cadavre glorieux et bruyant—pour un temps ridiculement court. Le petit garçon qui regardait la mort en face reste debout et intact—éternellement.
>
> C'est la vie qui l'aurait sans doute tué comme les autres. L'homme à la sentence, croyant le supprimer, l'a préservé. Quels que soient les mots dont il se grise, Créon joue toujours perdant. (Vandromme, p. 176)

Although it hardly does justice to Creon's position, this passage helps us to put the emphasis where Anouilh's play puts it: neither on the conscience of the King, as in the Greek play, nor exclusively on the heroine's martyrdom, but on the dramatic tension generated by a dialectical opposition: between the prosaic doctrine of devotion to duty and the sublime call to sacrifice oneself for an ideal, between rational acceptance and instinctive refusal, between life and death. It goes without saying that such an interpretation transcends the immediate context of 1942 or 1944; and while the cryptic *Angst* of *En attendant Godot*, or the even more cryptic metaphysics of some later examples of Absurdist drama, have proved not only a fashionable, but also a theatrically convincing, way of representing the post-war consciousness of the human predicament, Anouilh's rational debate, involving a more old-fashioned conflict of character in an intensely dramatic situation, is still an equally valid way of exploring the essential problem.

Of exploring—but of course without offering a solution. This is not drama with a message, whatever its first audiences may have been conditioned to believe; it does not use the facile stereotypes of melodrama for a propaganda purpose, and today's spectators and readers are able to observe the confrontation without taking sides. What may once have seemed the convincing expression of a political ideal is now revealed as possessing all the futility of an *acte gratuit*:

> Polynice n'était qu'un prétexte. Quand elle a dû y renoncer, elle a trouvé autre chose tout de suite. Ce qui importait pour elle, c'était de refuser et de mourir.

But if Antigone's gratuitous nihilism does not convince us of its validity in the real world—and the very fact that we are sitting in a warm theatre watching the play, or in a comfortable armchair reading Anouilh's text, shows that we have opted in practice for Creón's pragmatic alternative, and provisionally, at any rate, chosen the way of acceptance—perhaps we can say that it has the poetic force of a symbol, and that her suicidal revolt should be seen as the imaginative extension, rather than the literal expression, of the attitude she embodies.

If we are prepared to let the drama work on the level of imaginative suggestion rather than of rational persuasion, it is then, I am sure, that we shall be open to the full power of this remarkable play. Whether or not we can interpret this as a *tragic* quality is largely a question of definition. If we are looking for the metaphysical dimension of the Sophoclean drama, we shall not find it. The gods are absent from Anouilh's *Antigone*; and the intervention of the Prologue-Chorus does not necessarily produce a satisfactory substitute: does this feature in fact do any more than establish the play as 'metatheatre', the self-consciously theatrical product of the playwright's mind? For as H. Gignoux writes, commenting on le Choeur's 'C'est une question de distribution':

> Les rôles sont distribués par qui? Il ne semble pas qu'ils le soient, en l'espèce, par une divinité qu'on nous inviterait à prendre au sérieux . . . Puisque les puissances surnaturelles sont indifférentes ou absentes, et qu'il faut bien imputer cette 'distribution' à quelqu'un, il est permis de rendre responsable l'auteur lui-même usant de ses pleins pouvoirs, et de se demander alors si la fatalité qu'il fait peser sur ses personnages n'est pas l'effet des références littéraires dont il les entoure.

As Gignoux goes on to say, in what must still be one of the most perceptive analyses of Anouilh's play, it is not so much a question of the obvious reference to Sophocles as of the echoes of the playwright's own earlier theatre:

> Ce qui fait qu'[Antigone] se trouve en fin de compte dans un état d'esprit voisin de celui de Thérèse et d'Eurydice, c'est qu'elle envisage son avenir à la lumière de leurs passés; née du même père, sa mémoire est nourrie de leur expérience. (pp. 94–5)

Expressed as it is in the play, Antigone's nostalgic longing for the values of childhood and the past is not wholly convincing, since we know nothing of her childhood: it is something we have to take on trust; and Antigone's arbitrary self-absorption is matched by a similar self-centredness on the part of Créon. 'Ce ne sont plus deux affirmations qui s'affrontent', Gignoux suggests, 'mais deux négations'; and if this is capable of producing a fascinating psychological interplay, it lacks the positive values, the vision, that we look for in tragedy. 'Le drame psychologique accapare notre attention au détriment de la tragédie . . .', and the critic concludes that this is 'un drame psychologique en marge de la tragédie'. (pp. 113, 115)

This may well be true, and if one takes a rigorous, purist view of tragedy *Antigone* will no doubt fall short of the most exacting requirements. But if our criteria are less demanding, less traditionalist—if we are prepared to envisage a modern tragedy which reflects the anguish of twentieth-century man at the cruel absurdity of our existence in a godless world—then the moving spectacle of two characters, with both of whom we are encouraged to sympathize, locked in a 'dialogue de sourds' whose only possible outcome is death for one and defeat and loss for the other, must surely merit our consideration as an example of such a 'tragédie ontologique'[20].

Whether we are persuaded that it is a question of 'distribution' by some hostile fate—that Antigone, and Créon in his own way too, have personally been cast in the role of victims—or whether in some less specific way, making full allowance for the apparent free will enjoyed by both these intransigent characters, the dramatist is nevertheless suggesting that we are all of us victims of the 'absurd' universe in which we live: in either case the term 'tragedy' seems not inappropriate for a play which shows at every turn that human strength is so closely allied to human weakness, that triumph is merely another aspect of defeat, and that vulnerability and defencelessness are inescapable attributes of the human condition.

Notes

[1] The term 'trilogy' is to be avoided, as having a technical meaning in relation to Greek tragedy that does not fit the present case. It should be noted, moreover, that Sophocles did not compose the three plays in the order of their chronological sequence.

[2] An adaptation of Garnier's *Antigone* by Thierry Maulnier was performed in Paris in May 1944, in competition not only with Anouilh's play but also with Cocteau's version of Sophocles' text (with Honegger's music) at the Opéra. A critic wrote that 'Notre théâtre traverse aujourd'hui une crise aiguë d'antigonnite' (*Comoedia*, 15. v. 1944).

[3] 'Conférence prononcée à Athènes sur l'avenir de la tragédie' (1955) in *Théâtre, récits, nouvelles*, Paris, 1962, p. 1703.

[4] Line-references are to the Penguin Classics edition, trans. Watling.

[5] *Of Dramatic Poesy* (1668) in *Of Dramatic Poesy, and Other Critical Essays*, ed. G. Watson, London, 1962, I, p. 58

[6] I am grateful to my colleagues Professor John Gould and Dr Richard Buxton of the Department of Classics, University of Bristol, for kindly agreeing to read the material on Sophocles' *Antigone*.

7 Page-references throughout are to the edition by W. M. Landers, London 1957.

8 Though Anouilh uses both terms, I take it as self-evident that the two roles are one and the same. This corresponds to stage practice in presenting the play in the theatre.

9 André Barsacq, who directed the 1944 production, comments as follows: 'L'*Antigone* m'a permis de réaliser ce rêve que je caressais depuis si longtemps: concevoir une mise en scène d'où tout pittoresque serait banni, faire se dérouler l'action dans un décor neutre, une sorte de scène idéale qui donnerait une impression de grandeur par la seule noblesse de ses lignes' ('Lois scéniques', *Revue Théâtrale*, 5, April–May 1947, pp. 157–8).

10 Cf the comment made by editors of *L'Alouette*: 'In *Antigone*, for instance, we are made to feel that what we are watching is a play and nothing else, moreover that we are participating in it. Similarly in *L'Alouette* . . .' (*L'Alouette*, ed. M. Thomas and S. Lee, London, 1956, p. 16).

11 In *Ardèle* (1948). Cf. *Pièces grinçantes*, Paris, 1956, p. 64.

12 See the continuation of this passage quoted above, p. 20.

13 The name 'Jonas' is a strange choice. It corresponds to the Old Testament 'Jonah', and is hardly plausible as a modern French *nom de famille*; Camus was to use it as the name of the central character of one of the stories in *L'Exil et le royaume* (1957), but this was apparently in order to fit in with an epigraph taken from the Book of Jonah. Here, it may perhaps carry the popular connotation 'one who brings ill-luck'.

14 I am using the term current in French dramaturgical analysis to denote identifiable sections of a long scene. Here, the 'movements' indicate shifts in the audience's relationship with the characters.

15 *Le Rire* (1899), Paris, 1946, p. 39.

16 *Verweigerung oder Neue Ordnung: Jean Anouilhs 'Antigone' im politischen und ideologischen Kontext der Besatzungszeit 1940–1944*, 2 vols., Rheinfelden, 1982. Except where otherwise indicated, page-references in this chapter are to Dr Flügge's book, to which I am considerably indebted.

17 Quoted in P. Vandromme, *Jean Anouilh, un auteur et ses personnages*, Paris, 1965, pp. 175–6.

18 Cf. McIntyre, p. 154. The fragment is reproduced in R. de Luppé, *Jean Anouilh*, Paris, 1959, pp. 101–16.

19 I am excluding from consideration *Tu étais si gentil quand tu étais petit* (1969), in which Aeschylus' *Libation-bearers* is presented as a play within a play.

20 See I. Omesco, *La Métamorphose de la tragédie*, Paris, 1978.

Bibliography

Texts

J. Anouilh, *Antigone*, Paris (Table Ronde), 1946

    Nouvelles Pièces noires, Paris (Table Ronde), 1946

    Antigone, ed. W. M. Landers, London (Harrap), 1954

    Antigone, ed. J. Monférier, Paris (Bordas), 1968 (N.B.: this edition is abridged)

    Antigone (English translation by L. Galantière), New York (Samuel French), 1947

    Antigone (trans. Galantière) and *Eurydice*, London (Methuen), 1951

Sophocles, *The Theban Plays*, new translation by E. F. Watling, Harmondsworth (Penguin), 1947

Critical Studies

Beugnot, B. (ed.), *Les Critiques de notre temps et Anouilh*, Paris, 1977

Bowra, C. M., *Sophoclean Tragedy*, Oxford, 1944

Esslin, M., *The Theatre of the Absurd*, 1964

Flügge, M., *Verweigerung oder Neue Ordnung: Jean Anouilhs 'Antigone' im politischen und ideologischen Kontext der Besatzungszeit 1940–1944*, 2 vols., Rheinfelden, 1982

Frois, E., *Antigone: Profil d'une oeuvre*, Paris, 1972

Gignoux, H., *Jean Anouilh*, Paris, 1946

Hamburger, K., *Von Sophokles zu Sartre* (1962), trans. H. Sebba: *From Sophocles to Sartre*, New York, 1969

Harvey, J., *Anouilh: A Study in Theatrics*, New Haven and London, 1964

Howarth, W. D., 'Anouilh', *Forces in Modern French Drama*, ed. J. Fletcher, London, 1972, pp. 86–109

Ince, W. N., 'Prologue and Chorus in Anouilh's *Antigone*', *Forum for Modern Language Studies*, IV, 1968, pp. 277–84

John, S., 'Obsession and Technique in the Plays of Jean Anouilh', *French Studies*, XI, 1957, pp. 97–116

Kahl, D., *Die Funktionen des Rollenspiels in den Dramen Anouilhs*, Hamburg, 1974

Kitto, H. D. F., *Form and Meaning in Drama*, London, 1956

Luppé, R. de, *Jean Anouilh*, Paris, 1959

McIntyre, H. G., *The Theatre of Jean Anouilh*, London, 1981

Omesco, I., *La Métamorphose de la tragédie*, Paris, 1978

Pronko, L. C., *The World of Jean Anouilh*, Berkeley and Los Angeles, 1968

Rombout, A., *La Pureté dans le théâtre de Jean Anouilh*, Amsterdam, 1975

Sachs, M., 'Notes on the Theatricality of Jean Anouilh's *Antigone*', *The French Review*, XXXVI, 1962, pp. 3–11

Steiner, G., *The Death of Tragedy*, London, 1961

Vandromme, P., *Jean Anouilh, un auteur et ses personnages*, Paris, 1965

Waldock, A. J. A., *Sophocles the Dramatist*, Cambridge, 1966

Index